HUMAN RIGI

D0121175

WITHDRAWN

HUMAN RIGHTS IN ANOTHER KEY

Johan Galtung

Polity Press

First published in 1994 by Polity Press
in association with Blackwell Publishers.

Reprinted 2004

Editorial office:
Polity Press
65 Bridge Street
Cambridge CB2 1UR, UK

Marketing and production:
Blackwell Publishers
108 Cowley Road
Oxford OX4 1JF, UK

238 Main Street
Cambridge, MA 02142, USA

ISBN 0 7456 1375 6
ISBN 0 7456 1376 4 (pbk)

A CIP catalogue record for this book is available from the British Library and the Library of Congress.

Typeset in 10½ on 12pt Times
by Photoprint, Torquay, Devon

This book is printed on acid-free paper.

CONTENTS

PREFACE

For a peace researcher to be interested in human rights comes rather naturally. The overlap in value-orientation is obvious: human dignity, the use of normative power rather than sticks and carrots, the effort to reduce direct violence. My enthusiasm for that tradition, the glimmer of light even for the most tortured and utterly lonely prisoner, can be found all over in this book, even though, as a true friend, I try to focus constructively on the possible deficits.

I am grateful to many with whom I have been working on human rights problems over the last 20 years: Anders Wirak at the Chair of Peace and Conflict Research, University of Oslo; Peider Könz at the Inter-University Centre in Dubrovnik; Philip Alston, Steven Marks, and Christian Bay at the Goals, Processes and Indicators of Development Project of United Nations University; Asbjorn Eide of the Norwegian Institute for Human Rights; Oslo and Bernt Hagtvet of Chr. Michelsens Institute, Bergen, and Jon Van Dyke and Maivan Lam of the University of Hawaii, Honolulu. Also very useful were invitations from Antonio Cassese, Wolf Linder, and Georg Meggle to give human rights seminars at the Istituto Europeo Universitario, Firenze; Universität Bern and Universität des Saarlandes in Saarbrücken; and to Dieter Kinkelbur and Kuno Lorenz, Saar, for all their helpfulness, and to Torstein Eckhoff and Allan Rosas for very valuable comments.

The book is dedicated to the countless millions with their human rights infracted, willfully or not; as a tiny contribution to the great human rights tradition.

Johan Galtung
Honolulu and Versonnex

1

HUMAN RIGHTS AND THE WESTERN TRADITION

HUMAN RIGHTS: NORMS AND NORM-TRIADS

The purpose of this chapter is to contribute to the ongoing debate on human rights (HR), by exploring to what extent they are *Western*,[1] and what might be done to make them more *universal*. Whatever is Western, from Christianity via some of the colonial languages and Western science and technology to Western history and development models in general, tends to be conceived of as universal. The West is so powerful that such ideas as "Western history = universal history" and "Western culture = universal culture" are found not only among Westerners. The high level of acceptance of Western development models (called "modernization") implies an acceptance of the model character of both Western history and Western culture. Formulated in more Hegelian terms: there has been and still is an underlying assumption that humanity has had a crystallization point for early self-realization in the West. By implication, "Western HR = universal HR" has gained almost automatic acceptance.

But regardless of the strength of this tradition, pretending that something is universal does not make it universal in any operational or meaningful sense. Humanity is badly served if all shoe factories turn out shoes of size 40 and car factories cars for right-hand drive only. Simplifying to "universal = West + non-West", there are actually three problems here, not only that of imposing West on non-West when it does not fit, and not having non-West benefit from its own HR tradition. There is also the problem of the West not benefiting from the non-Western tradition. Loser: the whole world.

The reaction, or over-reaction to the present asymmetry could easily lead to an asymmetry with the three corresponding problems: imposing non-West on the West; not having the West benefit from its own tradition; and not having the non-West benefit from the (liberal) Western tradition. The last is often used as an argument not only against any change but against even looking into the problem. Those who argue that the HR tradition is Western are seen as arguing against the HR tradition in general; deliberately or not supporting repressive regimes in particular. The position taken here, however, is openness to all six problems. But given the Western background for the HR tradition the task right now is to analyze that tradition, and then bring in the non-West. Both–and, in other words.

The key entry points for discussing this problem are *time* in the sense of history as basic, i.e. structural, change, and *space* in the sense of culture. How did HR originate historically and grow structurally, and what kind of cultural imprint does the HR tradition carry? But first some conceptualization of HR is indispensable. A human right will be conceived of here as a norm, concerning, indeed protecting, the rock bottom of human existence. There is a link to basic human needs which potentially would make human rights applicable to human beings everywhere. As for any norms, there are norm-senders (S) who lay down the borderline between the pre-scribed, the indifferent, and the proscribed. There are norm-receivers (R) whose acceptance of the norm (meaning that the norm has been *received*, not only registered) implies inclusion of the prescribed and exclusion of the proscribed from their action repertoires. And there are norm-objects (O) – in principle the centerpiece of the construction – for whom a human right implies a claim on the norm-receivers if they omit the prescribed acts and/or commit the proscribed acts.

Today the norm-receivers are the states; the norm-sender is the community or organization of states, interpreted as the United Nations General Assembly (UNGA) for universal human rights; and the norm-objects are individual human beings.[2] The S, R, O-triad has a relatively steep gradient, sloping from a single UNGA via 189 UN member states (MS) to (soon) six billion individual human beings. Alternative S, R, O-triads can and should be imagined; some of them will be discussed in the final section of this chapter. But the final anchoring for human rights will be in norm-objects that are, usually, individual human beings.

Other S, R, O-triads in the UNGA–MS–human beings triangle are possible and meaningful. People, individually or collectively, also send these or similar norms to the state as a potential receiver: "Thou shalt not imprison me without due process of law," "Thou shalt provide me with gainful employment," and so on. Indeed, one of the pillars of democracy as a contract/covenant between "we, the people" and the state is the reception, by the state, of such norms, giving us the background for the HR tradition in the English (1688), American (1776/1787) and French (1789) revolutions. The use of UNGA as norm-sender for essentially the same norms in the Universal Declaration of Human Rights (1948) provided an extension mechanism for HR from the West to countries that did not have the HR tradition, e.g. because they never had similar (conservative, liberal) revolutionary or evolutionary processes, or had other revolutionary processes (struggles for independence from England, the United States and France; socialist revolutionary or evolutionary processes). Today only organizations of states are seen as legitimate norm-senders for not only negotiable but also ratifiable HR instruments, such as the instruments collected in the International Bill of Human Rights (the Universal Declaration of Human Rights; the International Covenant on Economic, Social and Cultural Rights and the International Covenant on Civil and Political Rights with Optional Protocol). And that leads to the two other triads with senders from below: individuals, groups and states sending HR norms to the UNGA, meaning the expectation that the UNGA will become norm-sender for new norms, propagated from below.

In the following there will be no hard, positivist assumptions about the "nature" of human rights except that ultimately they are supposed to serve basic human needs. The International Bill of Human Rights package is an outstanding achievement; but norms can be added to and subtracted from that package. In the process there will be other normative sources such as human needs and values from other civilizations. And the UNGA may not forever retain monopoly as universal norm-sender, nor the states as norm-receivers. In short, the human rights field remains open, meaning it is alive.

HUMAN RIGHTS: A HISTORICAL-STRUCTURAL PERSPECTIVE

National human rights can be seen as parts of a contract or covenant between the state and the human beings/citizens. For international human rights a three-tier world context with three constructs is needed: individuals, states, and communities/organizations of states. This particular social construction came slowly into being after the decline of the Middle Ages. The Westphalia *system* of 1648 and the Concert of Europe of 1815; the emergence of international governmental and people's organizations and of international law (the Hague system) in the nineteenth century building a *community* of states; and the *organizations* of the League of Nations (1919) and the United Nations (1945) serve as important stepping stones and convenient anchoring points for process analysis. If history is the record of social change and social change is interpreted as structural change, then there is not only a story but a history to be told here, and it has been told many times. Let me try a macro-historical version focusing on the processes relevant for the understanding of HR.

To start at one point: Reciprocal systems of rights and duties (obligations) must be as old as human beings themselves. The concrete normative content varies, with *lex talionis*, in positive or negative formulations or both, often used as a meta-norm. In *lex talionis*, Self-reference is the anchoring point for behavior towards Other. The bottom line of the ethical budget is what will ultimately benefit myself, in other words, the meta-norm is ego-centered: "Do unto others what you want others to do to you," or the same with negations.

But there is also a god-centered reference, probably equally universal. The question is what kind of god, what kind of theology as opposed to the anthropology underlying *lex talionis*. The distinction I shall use is between an immanent god inside us, making humans (in Buddhism all "sentient beings") imbued with that substance sacred; and a transcendental god outside, even outside Planet Earth (Thou who art in *Heaven*). In the immanent case the rights of Other and the duties of Self would be anchored in the unity of humans in addition to the sacredness of Other, and *lex talionis* comes in the back door through the assumption that hurting Other is also hurting Self. In the transcendental case the rights of Other and the duties of Self derive from the duties to a transcendental god, e.g. as formulated in the Judeo-Christian Ten Commandments (Exodus 20: 2–17, Deuteronomy 5: 6–21). There is still horizontal reciprocity, but not as a useful, well-tested traffic rule for human behavior or because unity of life implies symbiosis. The commandments are our duty to God as a vertical, transcendental ethics as opposed to horizontal, immanent ethics.

This logic is expressed with apodictic clarity in Matthew 25: 40 (positive version) and Matthew 25: 45 (negative version): When you did it to these my brothers you were doing it to me. When you refused to help the least of these my brothers, you were refusing help to me. Or, in the Latin version: *Quando non fecistis uni de minoribus his, nec mihi fecistis.*

This horizontal behavior is vertically anchored ethically.

But who is to judge? Ultimately *Thou* who art in heaven. But before that ultimate judgement his representatives, the clerical hierarchy. Being closest to a transcendental god they also came up on top of the social hierarchy when feudalism was crystallized during the "Middle Ages" (a rather strange term for a civilization describing itself as Christian, among other things referring to a time between two expansionist periods with strong state formations and rule by temporal powers). The abstract duty to the Father in Heaven was mirrored in the more concrete duty to the father in church.

The rest of the story can now be told quickly, using the principle of structural inertia or isomorphism through time. Two logically related processes took place: aristocracy replaced clergy on top of the social hierarchy and the top aristocrat, the king/emperor, took on god-like characteristics, being increasingly omnipresent, omniscient, and omnipotent (enlightened monarchy; absolutism). This does not mean that clergy and god came second in the temporal order constituted by aristocracy and king, but that they constituted a spiritual order on a side-track, no longer in the center of society. The relative significance of the two orders then becomes the focus of politics, the trend being secularization, implying increasing marginalization both of clergy and god, even to the point of the latter being declared dead or at least dying. Conceivably this is what happened in the Soviet Union under perestroika, with the second, ideological order, the Party, being marginalized and even history, the homologue of god, receding into the background and the old god coming up again.

Transition formulas were found and are still used. The king became *rex gratia dei*, and theology (Luther) produced the teaching of the two orders, *die zwei Regimenten*, essentially reproducing the clever biblical distinction between what is of Caesar and what is of God, with the admonition to give unto each his due. Gradually the king and aristocracy were then replaced by cabinet and bureaucracy, meaning the state (transition formula: *l'état, c'est moi*); with the old order, the *ancien régime*, marginalized if they were not executed (French and Russian revolutions). What remained was and is the essence, the structural relation between state and citizen being patterned on the relation between God and Christian. That these two transformations replacing entrenched powers were not easy is borne out clearly by the drama of European history. They would have been considerably more problematic had isomorphism not been preserved. *Plus ça change, plus c'est la même chose*: the actors change, but the structure remains the same. The essence of a crime such as murder is no longer against God but against the state (or "the people", as represented by the state); the victim comes second. The state is not merely a third party but is directly offended, and like God entirely justified in administering punishment; "doing it to me."

The king being only a local *primus inter pares* and the state being one among several, however, neither king nor state could be more than local gods, however omnipresent, omniscient, and omnipotent. The search for a single and universal super-king and/or super-state still continues. Napoleon, refusing to be crowned by the pope, placing the crown on himself, tried to cast himself in the first role. The United Nations has been cast in the second. US resistance to the UN might be understood not only as power struggle in the temporal order between US and UN, but also as a US refusal to let the UN play god-like roles, thereby replacing the spiritual order (in which the US, as God's own country, may feel it is more deeply embedded with nothing in between). But with the UN system both norm-sender and norm-receivers were in place, US misgiving notwithstanding.

We still have to account for the third construct, the individuals, in whom the rights are vested, as norm-objects. Imagine a hunter-gatherer, or pastoral nomadic community with people woven together in structures that take the shape of nets of rights and duties. The interaction net is made in such a way that everybody is relatively well protected. Human beings are of course physically/biologically recognizable in this network. And the more densely the net is spun, the more difficult or meaningless will it be to detach the individual from the network. Individuals are in the *net* not only in the *knot*, a useful metaphor and vocabulary.[3]

Individualizing Judaism/Christianity/Islam with a transcendental god emphasizes the knots, and union-orientated Hinduism/Buddhism with a more immanent god-concept the nets. Transcendental religions endow human beings with individual souls as that which can attain union with god. Immanent religions depend less on that concept, which is rejected out of hand in radical Buddhism. But occidental religions also have immanent, net-orientated, collectivist aspects. There was also legitimation from below in the voice of the people, with *vox populi, vox dei* as the obvious transition formula, meaning that God also speaks through the people. And the whole tradition of democracy took shape and is still taking shape.

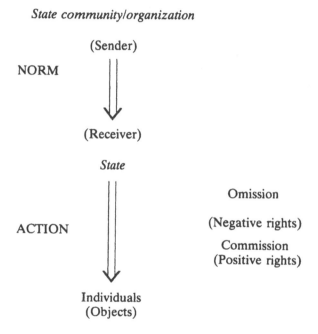

Figure 1.1 The normative structure of human rights

The relations between individuals within a state were increasingly regulated by national (or "municipal") laws, and between states increasingly through international law. It is in this context that human rights should be seen: as an imaginative complex construct *combining* elements of national and international law. Human rights are based on both of them and contribute to both of them. In the three-tier system indicated we get something like figure 1.1. The human rights in figure 1.1 are implemented as concrete actions engaged in by the state. They are of two kinds, the negative human rights focusing on the proscribed acts the state should abstain from, i.e. on domesticating, restraining the state, making the state obey due process of law in principle created and upheld by the state. And then there is the second kind, the prescribed acts of commission the state should engage in. The negative human rights limit *l'état gendarme*, the positive human rights define *l'état providence*, the state as a provider, with the individuals having claims *on* the state, not only *against* the state as for the negative rights.

The civil and political rights are often seen as being more of the first kind, and the economic, social and cultural rights as more of the second. The original French *Déclaration du droit de l'homme et du citoyen* of 1789, and the Universal Declaration of Human Rights of 10 December 1948, can be seen as combining the two elements, and that also applies to the two Covenants of 16 December 1966. But the balance between focus on acts of omission and acts of commission moved in the direction of the latter, supported by the idea of an increasingly interventionist state. The latter extends the contractual power of the state as provider, one reason why one of these Covenants is not yet ratified by the US, and one reason why this trend may now be reversed (for some time).

However, this distinction is less important and also mainly semantic, like the distinction between "freedom from" and "freedom to," much depending on what kind of words are used and whether or not negative particles are made use of. More important is the *social* structure of a human right. An effort to develop an image is given in figure 1.2.

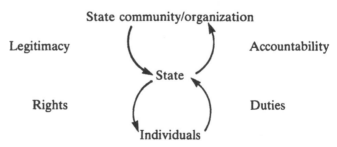

Figure 1.2 The social structure of human rights

The very term "human rights" focuses our attention on human individuals and on something called rights. The right is then conceived of as wrested from or conceded by the state, whether it is called "inherent" and "inalienable" or not. However, any social system analysis between actors organized in two or three tiers would cry eloquently for some image of reciprocity. If the state gives or concedes "rights" to individuals, what must the individuals give back to the state in return? And whatever it is, could this not possibly be called (human) "duties"?[4]

I shall call them human *duties*, indicating that the very phrase "human rights" is actually a misnomer for the more complete, but awkward, "human rights/duties." "Human rights" may even be seen as a propaganda formulation, relatively similar (and not by chance) to the phrasing used in economic theory when economists talk about "goods and services" and never about "bads and disservices." State and capital may both prefer to be represented by mystifying euphemisms. And the fundamental thesis of this section is that any single-minded focus on human *rights*, and not on duties, is like reading one side of an insurance contract, overlooking the small print on the reverse. There is actually a warning against this reading of the Universal Declaration in article 29.[5]

Correspondingly, the state is embedded in a state system, which may or may not give rise to a community or even an organization of states. The state organization is only a norm-sender if the state, at least to some extent, makes itself *accountable* to the state organization, which implies readiness to be evaluated by the norms it has agreed to receive, the human rights norms. The question is what the state receives in return for making itself accountable. The answer suggested in figure 1.2 is "legitimacy," bestowed upon the state by the state community. Here we could imagine a process. The state community accepts a new state and confers on it status as a *bona fide* member of the state system. The new member will immediately be exposed to the human rights norms, and since these are institutionalized norms, no matter how weak, an element of accountability is established. With increasing accountability/fulfillment there will be increasing legitimacy. Of the two, accountability and fulfillment, the former is probably more important than the latter. A state may have a high level of fulfillment but make itself impenetrable to outside scrutiny. On the other hand, states may also make themselves fully accountable, exposing all their failures and shortcomings. The latter is probably more a member of the system than the former, subjecting itself to review. In accountability there is a heavy element of submissiveness dear to the norm-sender/law-giver. Fulfillment without accountability smacks of arrogance; of being accountable only to oneself. Even more arrogant would be accountability while at the same time refusing to receive the norms from the organization of states and receiving them from elsewhere, including being one's own norm-sender.

Thus, there is a complicated balance at work here. Human rights should not be identified with an individual right merely because the norm-object is an individual. Located in the interface between international and national law, in a sense as customary parts of both of them, the human rights serve an important integrative function in the total world normative system by tying the three tiers together.

Again, we cannot go further in the exploration of this phenomenon without looking at the *duties*. Between the emerging state and the emerging individuals a new *contrat social* was forged. We have seen nothing like the end of that process yet. But one key to the phenomenon is found precisely in the title of the original French document, referring not only to the rights of "man," but also to the rights of "citizen." A "man" stands for a *person* in a more absolute, perhaps even universal sense, whatever that might mean. But he or she is a citizen only relative to his or her own state, and more particularly to the state of which he or she is a citizen. The duties that immediately come to one's mind would be the duty (particularly of men) to produce and (particularly of women) to reproduce; in other words, to make the state rich in terms of non-human and human capital. Then there is the economic duty to pay taxes and the political duty to be law-obedient, or at least not to work against the political machinery. And finally there is the military duty (particularly for men) to sacrifice one's own life, for the cause defined by the state (meaning the cabinet government) in the interstate system.

These are heavy duties; the last – to lay down one's own life – even extreme. It is important to see the rise of obligatory war service, from pertaining only to a caste of warriors to affecting all able-bodied men and women, and ultimately involving everybody as non-protesting victims in increasingly totalizing wars, in the light of increasing scope for human rights.[6] *Total rights in principle entitle the state to demand total duties in return.* The total provider is entitled to total commitment. The state finally gives emancipation to women, but the state takes it back as military service. *The state giveth, the state taketh, the name of the state be praised*, for this is where the god-like substance has been transferred. Basic question: is this a good deal?

In this process the state has a very rational argument: "if I, the state, am to provide for all items in these international checking lists of rights, then I simply need more resources." For this to happen the citizens have to work hard, producing a surplus, directly and indirectly, that can be used to provide for what not only the citizens but the whole world system demands of the state. The citizen would have the duty to provide the state with the means with which the state can provide for the citizen and fulfill its obligation to the state system; and the duty to make use of his or her rights, to claim but not to over-claim, thereby legitimizing further the calls to duty from the state. He or she will not be able to extricate himself from the duties by not claiming the rights. Refusal to go to school cannot be exchanged for refusal to do military service. A right implies the duty to claim that right. Not to claim the right destroys the construction of the right as natural, inborn, inalienable. And reduces the credit due to the state for implementing the norms.

This is important because it also serves to illustrate why there is no contradiction between a state being high in fulfillment of human rights for the citizens and at the same time highly aggressive in the interstate system, with a high level of ability to mobilize the citizens for that type of aggression. I am actually thinking both of the United States (relatively high on civil/political rights) and of the former Soviet Union (relatively high on social/economic rights) in this connection. They both worked out contracts with their citizens. And they both succeeded, to some extent, in making the citizens pay less attention to the neglected human rights (high level of unemployment in the United States, and misery; high level of political repression in the Soviet Union) because so much else was relatively well provided for.[7] There may be other states in the world system with a very low level of provision for any kind of right, and consequently also unable to mobilize their population unless they have other sources to draw upon, such as normative power in the shape of intact religious myths and beliefs, and visions of missionary rights and duties. With the human rights a contractual rather than a normative basis for mobilizing the population was/is institutionalized as a very powerful way of exchanging rights for duties. The individual has a claim on the state, and so has the state on the individual.

However that may be, there can be no doubt that human rights as an institution are linked to a particular historical phase in the evolution in the West of the modern state system. More particularly, they are linked to a strong and central state with considerable resources at its disposal, otherwise many of the rights – the implementation of which could be quite costly – simply become vacuous. What emerges is a powerful provider in our midst, some kind of latter-day god, not only omnipresent, omniscient and omnipotent, but also benevolent, as a welfare state, *l'état providence* (as opposed to *l'état gendarme*) should be. Human rights balance omniscience and omnipotence with benevolence, of the negative and positive kinds mentioned. But as the construction has emerged, state omniscience and omnipotence come as parts of the bargain. With obedient citizens dutifully claiming their rights and exercising their duties they can become quite formidable in their consequences. Till we wake up one day, realizing that total freedoms, in the shape of rights, have made us totally unfree, trapped by duties. And not only in bondage to the state, but also to an organization of states that bestows legitimacy on a state that bestows rights on its citizens – in return for accountability and duties. Weber's iron cage? Giddens's surveillance society? The question remains: Is this a good deal?

To summarize: what is Western about this construction generated by Western history is not the content of the norms (to be discussed in the next section), but the construction itself:

1 the norm-triad gradient expresses the vertical slope of an ethics of rights and duties from above rather than human compassion;
2 the construction gives the universal and regional organizations of states increasing legitimacy, leading to a more centralized world society;
3 the construction gives the state increasing legitimacy, leading to a more centralized national society;
4 the construction detaches the individual knot even more from nets of reciprocity and solidarity, leading to more alienation.

HUMAN RIGHTS: A CIVILIZATIONAL-CULTURAL PERSPECTIVE

The approach taken in this section will be less historical, more synchronous, seeing Western civilization as one major *macro-culture*, among others. The question to be answered is to what extent, and precisely how, the content of the human rights as we know them in their totality serves as a carrier of Western civilization as opposed to other civilizations, with a relatively clearly expressed and consistent Western bias. The question to be asked is not whether this is good or bad; only whether it is the case. Evaluation and "what can be done about it" come later.

For the exploration of this problem a vision of Western civilization is needed. The present vision is based on cosmology analysis.[8] Civilizations are then explored along seven dimensions for their assumptions about space, time, knowledge, nature, persons, societies, and the transpersonal, the last in the West meaning *God*. The particular stand taken by Western civilization along these seven dimensions is indicated as hypotheses, and what then follows is an exploration of the extent to which human rights can be seen as an exemplification of that particular civilizational position.

Let us look at them quickly so as to get an overview.

Space The Western assumption is that the world can be divided into three parts: a center, which is in the West; a periphery waiting to receive whatever comes from the West; and a recalcitrant evil refusing to receive the word, and the goods and services that follow, and to be incorporated as second-class West (for them harsher treatment may be in order). In this image of the spatial arrangement of the world there are actually three ideas: *centralism*, with the West as the causal center of the world; *universalism*, with the idea that what is good for the West is good for the world; and a *good/evil dichotomy* marginalizing evil, trying to beat evil with crusades or deter it with atom bombs.

The human rights tradition can be seen in this light. As argued in the preceding section, not only did it originate historically in the West and has been propagated from the West, the tradition could only have originated in the West. The Universal Declaration of Human Rights was accepted by a predominantly Western United Nations and might have faced many more problems in Vienna in 1993. In the first years it was disseminated and propagated, and still is, from the West towards the rest of the world. In the Cold War, dominating East–West relations during almost the entire period since the 1948 Universal Declaration, the civil and political human rights on which the West sees itself as being particularly strong have been emphasized more than the social and economic rights where the socialist countries tended to see themselves as stronger. And most Western countries rank above most Third World countries on both kinds of human rights.

Whatever the reason may be, one more dimension has been institutionalized whereby the center can remain the center and the periphery the periphery. This enables countries in the West to appoint themselves judges over the rest of the world, distributing certificates of high and low levels of fulfillment. The objection to this argument would be that the West simply *is*, as also evidenced by the fact that there are more people wanting to migrate into the West than into other parts of the world.[9] And the counter-objection is that this is so because the West has the power to define what is "best." The obvious hypothesis is that a norm (such as right to care for the aged within the family itself, as opposed to old-age homes) more adhered to in the non-West than in the West would have a hard time being accepted as a "human right" as long as the West has the power to prevent it. The Third World might rank higher, and the West does not appreciate that. Moreover, wealth is always attractive.

Time The Western time perspective combines progress with asymptotic convergence to an ideal *Endzustand*, possibly with a crisis before that state of affairs is attained. The human rights conceptualization is to a large extent of that kind. There seem to be two processes at work. On the one hand, there is a given set of human rights and the painstaking, sometimes quick, sometimes slow, process of states fulfilling the norms, hopefully converging asymptotically to that ideal world. But there is also the second process of expanding the set of norms, identifying new human rights, institutionalizing them, thereby modeling Utopian society through a process of norm expansion. Combined, these two processes will always cement the leadership of the leaders, by definition already fairly high on implementing norms. But seeing others catching up they can still retain leadership of and distance from other countries (essential in a center–periphery conceptualization of the world) by adding new rules to the game. At the end of the process is Utopia with all rights fulfilled all over. The process gives to the center the right to define what Utopia looks like. And the Western center will tend to define it in such a way that they themselves are given permanent residency, or at least the first position on the waiting line.

Knowledge The Western knowledge structure is atomistic and deductive, as opposed to the holistic/dialectic combination that can be found in many other cultures. The fragmentary, atomistic aspect is reflected in two ways: the individual as the unit of norm fulfillment, as opposed to the group, and the single human rights norm as the unit of account. Instead of holistic judgements of whole countries as "Christian" or "civilized" comes the atomistic and empirical mapping of human rights fulfillment for m individuals on n variables of human rights. The matrix is formidable, like an enormous chessboard where red lights indicate deficiencies to be eliminated through adequate norm enforcement. Again this is not a question of good or bad, only of noting an unmistakably Western epistemology at work with the great attention given to the social atom, the individual; and to the conceptual atom, the specific HR variable. At the world level the atom is the country, not the system.

Nature The Western perspective is that of *Herrschaft* over nature, meaning that humans have the right to manipulate nature more or less as they want. Nature exists *für mich*, not *an sich*. One particular aspect of this is the unlimited right to kill animals for human consumption, even to expose them to highly painful "experiments," presumably for human betterment through insight gained in matters relating to health and disease. Humans are the end; nature is means. Animals and plants do not have legal standing, hence no rights.[10]

This anthropocentric perspective is fully reflected in the human rights tradition, even in the very name, "human rights." Animal rights are now (jokingly) being considered. Nature's rights might be around the corner,[11] but they are late in coming, possibly too late to save important species. Moreover, who will be the norm-senders when the directly concerned parties – animals and plants – are not articulating in a manner understandable to the norm-receivers, the states? Articulation has to be mediated through human beings, such as animal and nature lovers, and their articulation may be far from reliable. Leaving that point aside, it is clear that in the lack of consideration for non-human nature a position has been taken, and that position is in agreement with Western civilization in general. The human rights as they emerged remain anthropocentric.

Persons The Western position, in Freudian terms is based on strong egos (individualism); sometimes using (moral) superegos to control the id, their bodies, sometimes the other way round; the "ideational" and the "sensate" as Sorokin refers to them in *Social and Cultural Dynamics*. The common element is the sense of ownership of the body, and an individual relation to the superego, privatizing both the body and the superego. From this follow two important aspects of the Western approach, the sacredness of the individual body, and spirit of the individual.

Societies The Western position combines verticality and post-medieval individualism in a strongly competitive system defining winners and losers. The model sketched above of the human rights concept reinforces that structure. There is the primacy of the national and international levels over the local level. Individuals are subjected to the state as citizens (subjects), even if entitled to human rights in return. However, with perhaps as much as 90 percent of the global economic assets centrally controlled inside states, and most of the remaining decision-making at the international level, almost nothing is left to the local level (because local assets are small and ultimately tied up with central decisions). With this pattern repeated in administrative and political decisions verticality certainly has some backing in reality. A focus on the word "right" alone makes it not look like that; coupled with the word "duty" it becomes more clear.

But this verticality is found in most social constructions. What makes for Westernness is the way it is coupled to individualism in strongly competitive relations. Human rights become individual rights to the extent that individuals are the norm-objects, the units to which the norms are related and in which they are ultimately fulfilled. This excludes collective rights such as peoples' rights and other group rights. Women, age groups, indigenous groups, ancient peoples, non-Western cultures pocketed inside Western societies are such groups, at the bottom of society often engaged in efforts to imitate the states subjugating them. More than most, they are in need of human rights protection to preserve and enhance their *group* characteristics, not only as individuals inside a given social structure. Denial of such collective rights is verticality at work. The individualizing prospect of human rights deprives these underprivileged groups as such of their major political asset: mobilization and organized struggle *as a group*. In some cases their grievances may be adequately redressed by extending individual rights. Group rights become a matter of urgency the moment the group as a whole wants something different from what can be granted to the sum of individuals, such as national sovereignty under the doctrine of national self-determination, the only collective right that seems to be solidly enshrined. All these struggles have been and are uphill.

This has an important consequence. The individualizing condition for benefiting from the rights is not only that people reciprocate with duties, but also that they accept the rights as individuals, not as groups. The right to education means each individual's right to have access to the public schools as defined by and organized by the state, and as run by the dominant (majority or not) group. It does not necessarily mean the right of a group of individuals with some shared (ascribed or achieved) characteristics to institutionalize their own type of education. The only exception would be in connection with religion and language, for a very simple reason: they are the raw material out of which most nation states are wrought, which is the reason urgent group claims have to be met at some point. Failure to implement these rights easily leads to an explosive situation. But teaching the vernacular is still not the same as teaching in the vernacular, and this is where the state often draws the line. Here, not a step further.

As rights are also coupled with such duties as taxation and conscription (according to the argument above) to enable the state to do what the state deems necessary in order to secure the rights, the question of reciprocity arises. Thus, if money is needed for the welfare state then the state might believe in hydro-electric plants in order to provide energy cheaply in a marketable form, and to make a profit on the sale of that energy. In doing so the state might act against the interests of such groups as native populations or "nature lovers." But as there are (almost) no group rights, only individual rights, for humans in general and for categories, there is at present no way in which this would be rejected as counteracting human rights. Individual members of a native group more deprived than the average may secure legal redress on the basis of human rights. Not the group as an organization; mainly the category of individuals.[12] The state would tend not to like group rights standing in the way of the nation-building enterprise, preferring direct lines of command to the social atoms, the individuals.

The transpersonal The Western perspective also presupposes an overriding, transcendental principle. It was god in the old days; one or more of the successors to god nowadays. These successors, as argued above, were the king, the state, the people, and the state organization (the League of Nations, the United Nations, etc.). The state is then constructed in the image of a benevolent, omnipresent, omniscient and omnipotent king, possibly receiving legitimacy both from the state community and from the people. The human rights tradition contributes to this construction as the enlightened state receives an increasing number of norms, implements them in the form of human rights, and is even able to extract such duties from the citizenry as being compliant hostages to nuclear deterrence, meaning potential collective extermination. The new *contrat social* looks like the old one with allegiance to the *Obrigkeit*, the authority, in return for protection and assistance. The state elevates itself through an act of levitation to the transcendental levels of even deciding over omnicide, through weapons of mass destruction, while standing on top of a growing human rights mountain.

It is not where the human rights are located on any single one of these seven dimensions that counts. It is the whole package that is unmistakably Western. Propagation of human rights, consequently, is also propagation of Western civilization, and partly intended as such. This in itself does not make the Western human rights tradition wrong. But it certainly leads to two important questions. What, if anything, is so specifically Western that it should not form part of a *universal* declaration? And what could other civilizations, major or minor by today's thinking, contribute to a universal declaration? The questions are not new. But the failure to address them effectively is problematic, to say the least.

The problems: ten pointers to the future

Let us first ask the question: what are the concrete consequences of this massive Western structural/cultural export in terms of contradictions that have shown up, and may sooner or later show up more clearly, both within and between states, and ultimately for individuals? The answer has to be ambivalent:

1   a system for increasing protection and provision for increasing numbers of individuals on an increasing number of HR dimensions;
2   the reinforcement of centralizing tendencies both in world, regional and national societies, based on a vertical reciprocity imposing accountability on states and duties on the citizens within an increasingly homogenizing world culture; and
3   the destruction of alternative structures and cultures; as a consequence of the four structural problems listed on page 12 and the seven cultural export problems in the preceding section; eleven in total.

Accepting the first consequence but not the other two, the problem is how to address them without losing what has been gained. This may look formidable the way it has been formulated, but actually directs our attention, in a relatively systematic manner, to concrete problems for which solutions may exist if not today then tomorrow. Some of them are already being contemplated.

The problem of the steep norm-triad gradient   The solution does not lie in the abolition of the UNGA–state–individual triad, but in surrounding it with other triads. Limiting ourselves to mundane, not transcendental, actors we could divide norm-senders and norm-receivers into universal, regional, national, sub-national (group), and individual. If we assume that the norm-object remains the individual, and that the purpose of the whole construction is to safeguard basic human needs, then we get $5 \times 5 = 25$ different norm-triads, with universal–national–individual as the only triad used to construct human rights today. If we assume that the norm-object also could be groups, opening for collective rights, then we get an additional 25; 50 in all. That gives us a lot of possibilities. Let us look at some of them.

Obviously, "universal" as sender has already been interpreted to mean UN organizations other than the UNGA, such as UNESCO, WHO, FAO, ILO and UNICEF to take some examples relating directly to more specific human needs. And "regional" as sender has been interpreted to mean Europe, Africa, and the Pacific. These interpretations could also apply to the receiver side, with the UNGA in fact saying that in addition to the states, Specialized Agencies and the regions should also be responsible for the enactment of human rights. Moreover, these two approaches could increasingly be combined. They are both minor variations within the present human rights discourse and structure and should not encounter resistance for reasons of structure, only when new content is introduced. According to the general theory above, such changes would give more authority to other parts of the UN and to regions, thereby decentralizing along functional and geographical lines, not concentrating the ultimate, universal normative emission in one sender (UNGA), and the delicate balance between enacting rights and cashing in on duties in one receiver only (the state).

However, more interesting innovative combinations could be explored. In line with a tendency found many places in the world towards devolution within the state, how about leaving the task of enacting some rights to the local level, provinces, or even to municipalities? This would be in line with the philosophy underlying (subsidiary) federalism, and again in line with strong political traditions. There is also the possibility of being more flexible, leaving to the local population to decide who should be the norm-receiver. If the choice is in favor of a subnational unit then that unit would have a direct link to the norm-sender, bypassing the nation state, a formula that would loosen world society, making it more similar to national societies with multiple channels of command and communication.

The problems appear the moment we consider senders and receivers that are non-territorial, nonstate, like international peoples' organizations (IPOs) and transnational corporations (TNCs), and senders that are interest groups, national or inter/transnational, such as occupational groups (trade unions), age and gender groups, racial and ethnic groups. And yet, why could not TNCs be given the task of implementing some basic human needs in addition to, or instead of, some of the things they are doing? If successful they would benefit even if they have to pay the price of making themselves more accountable. In line with the general arguments the point is not to let the state off the hook of accountability, but to extend accountability to other world actors. The point is not that the UNGA should cease norm-production, but that several major organizations could send universal (not only regional) norms with human rights status when, for instance, the Catholic Church is doing so. ILO is a good, positive example.

Would this not add up to too many norms from too many sources? People raised in monotheistic cultures with one spiritual authority would be predisposed to agree; others might have more training in moral diversity. The argument would be that it is in our interest to spin a dense normative web of norms by and large pointing in the same (basic human needs) direction, dispersing both authority and credit. Above all this is an argument in favor of taking *civil society* seriously, not only the three-tier state construction based on the state system.

The problem of world power concentration   The problem is not a world central authority able to disburse goods and services, but a world government with heavy machinery for coercive enforcement and a singular, universalistic world culture. Projecting from nation states, some conclude that this would be the solution, not contemplating the amount of coercive machinery needed to extract compliance from recalcitrant states, or whether punishment as a means of securing general and individual prevention of crimes will work any better at the international than the national levels. Multiplying senders and receivers is probably the best antidote to over-centralization. And the notion of universal human rights essentially drawn from only one civilization with one sender only, UNGA, with a Security Council (Western dominated) equipped to enforce compliance, is a recipe for regional and national revolts. The similarity with the Christian Crusades (1095–1291) is only too obvious.

The problem of national power concentration Here some fairly concrete suggestions can be made. If the problem is that rights too easily translate into implicit duties, then the solution is to make those duties explicit and challenge them! Two such duties were mentioned above: taxation and conscription; the former challenged by the right, the latter by the left. We could easily imagine two new human rights here: the right of the individual to refuse military service, and the right of the individual to strike a bargain with the state, unpackaging the state package of services, accepting (and paying) for some, rejecting (and not paying) for others (like insurance policies). A deconstruction not only of the state discourse but of the state itself, in other words.

The problem of individual alienation Again, no simple institutional solution is around the corner. What we are looking for is the dense cocoon of a net of reciprocal rights and duties, from individuals, to individuals, and about individuals. Neither "rights only" nor "duties only" will do. The general word is *compassion*, within a unity-of-being ethos, a relatively clear normative content in some fields, and ethical intuition in the rest. In short, a richer ethical culture than we have in many places of the world today where waning faith in God as the ultimate norm-sender has coincided with waxing alienation not only from the human Other, but also from Self.

The problem of balanced normative input The Judeo-Christian normative culture is richly represented in the HR tradition. Three contributions stand out: the sacredness of the individual human body (against torture, for instance), the sacredness of the individual human spirit (against repression of expression and impression, for instance) and equal treatment, regardless of gender, race, class, nation.

These are major inputs to a universal normative culture. Moreover, they can also be used against toxic pollution (industry) to the body, and spiritual pollution (mass media) to the spirit.

But how about Islam? How could an institution like the *zakat*, making individual almsgiving for the satisfaction of the basic needs of others an obligation, be fitted into the scheme? In that case the norm-receiver would be the individual, as would also the norm-object. The norm-sender for the Muslim is Allah. But why not let the UN reproduce an Islamic norm for the benefit of non-Muslims?

In a similar vein, a very important normative culture could be lifted from Hinduism-Jainism-Buddhism (particularly the last two): *ahimsa*, non-violence. Why should not states and others, as norm-receivers, be given the task of working systematically for the reduction of violence of all kinds when they are given the task of working systematically for the reduction of disease of all kinds? Particularly as violence is becoming a major cause of death. Because the state wants to retain its monopoly on physical violence in its power repertory for internal or external use, but not disease (hence a certain aversion to biological and chemical warfare because they kill through disease-like processes)?

Correspondingly, from the Chinese tradition could come a respect for the family as a unit, partly by having the family as a norm-receiver for basic needs provision, partly by having the family as a norm-object to be protected by the state. And from the Japanese tradition could come a point that might sound like a joke but is not: the right *not* to have vacation. In a more serious vein: how could the famous article 9 of the Japanese Constitution ("the Japanese people forever renounce war as a sovereign right of its nation and the threat or use of force as means of settling international disputes") become a part of world culture? Japan wants to be equal, but why not try to raise others to the Japanese constitutional level rather than lower Japan to their level by circumventing article 9? Even if article 9 was forced upon them by the victor rather than emerging out of the Japanese tradition? The answer is not found in the UN Charter with its two-tier normative structure; the sender being the San Francisco Conference (26 June 1945) and the receivers, the member states. The interesting construction would be to introduce the UNGA as norm-sender for article 9, with a blank instead of the word "Japanese," and then use the citizens of any country as norm-receivers controlling the war-renunciation that is in fact realized by the state, which then becomes the norm-object. Are we ready?

And then there are the countless "minor" cultures; indigenous, native. We are still rich. But we are undermining that richness by reducing the cultural and structural diversity in the world just as we are reducing the bio-diversity needed for ecological balance. The meta-norm would be to preserve and increase cultural and structural diversity so that an ever richer human rights tradition could be created.

The problem of the Endzustand   The *Endzustand*, the final state, assumes our ability today to have an image of the end of the process. If there is one thing we can learn from history, a good example would be that this ability is limited, or zero. Like any process the HR process is filled with contradictions, and we ourselves are parts of that contradiction. At the roots of positivism as epistemology lies the idea that the future is built into the present; at the roots of dialectics the notion of reality as self-transcending into new phases/stages that are not only unknown but also unknowable (if we knew them we would already be halfway there). Hard positivism, in the sense just defined, would have to be rejected. A softer positivism, however, assuming that we have to work from where we are and that the near future is relatively knowable on that basis, becomes more acceptable.

The problem of atomism/deductivism   This is less of a problem. The issue can be formulated very simply: do we or do we not know what we are doing when we are propagating human rights? What is the "essence" of the HR exercise? The flat operational answer, "The International Bill of Human Rights," defines the exercise in extension but not in intention. The "essence" as seen by the present author lies in the relation to basic human needs. The beautifully structured text by McDougal, Lasswell, and Chen[13] defines eight areas – respect, power, enlightenment, well-being, wealth, skill, affection, and rectitude (sometimes adding security) – which could be fitted into basic needs categories. What matters is not the number, or the term, but the willingness to develop a discourse both at the atomistic (the single norms) and the holistic (packages of norms) levels. Both will always have to be revised, but then we at least know what we are trying to revise.

The problem of anthropocentrism   There are, of course, two very different ways of approaching the problem of animal and plant rights: extension of compassion to all sentient beings, i.e. the unity-of-life principle, regarding them as sacred because they possess life; and an indirect *lex talionis*, "do (don't do) unto animals/plants so that they can (cannot) continue serving you." The perspectives can be referred to as biocentric and homocentric respectively, and it is not obvious that they exclude each other. Immanent Buddhism would tend to favor the former, the occidental transcendental religions the latter, since they are homocentric. In either case non-human forms of life would be included as norm-objects; in other words, a major change of the norm-triad. We are probably not ready for it yet, but we might see the homocentric perspective as a start, keeping biocentric rooting for later (but not too much later).

The problem of the strong egos   As mentioned, this is seen as the source of valuable Western contributions to a world dialogue, with give-and-take aiming at truly universal human rights (so far we have heard only from the West). But precisely these strong Western egos may be insensitive to the softer voices from the subjugated discourses of the weaker egos.

The problem of social individualism   This is the problem of group rights, with groups as norm-objects, ultimately also as norm-receivers. As argued in the preceding section, the problem is whether the group rights differ from the aggregate or sum of individual rights. If they do not differ no problem arises; individualism prevails. If they differ, the group running the state will prefer the aggregate of individual rights in order to assimilate the group into the dominant (majority or not) structure and culture. If the subjugated group still insists on group rights, then the *actio popularis* is at least potentially available and may last forever. Finally, if there are no individual rights counterparts the group right may sail through easily. The classical example is national self-determination, with no individual counterpart. And as to the opposite case (no group rights counterpart), most civil and political rights may serve as an example. The freedom of expression, for instance, is clearly the aggregate of individual freedoms as only individuals express themselves.

But this does not work for many of the social, economic and cultural rights. Access to the schools run by the dominant group is not the same as running schools oneself, perhaps not as deep as the difference between some other group's religious service and one's own, but in that general direction. There is a difference between access to the dominant system of health care and running one's own health-care system; all of this because the faith in a universally valid curriculum and a universally valid health care is challenged, like the faith in a universally valid religion.

And, possibly the most important one: the difference between group property and the aggregate of individual property; the latter is the famous right to have private property, the former is "collectivism," common property, *res communis*. In all probability this is the most sticky issue, the script underlying them all, informing people whether they should oppose or endorse group rights. Recognition of groups other than nations (with the right to own states) might lead to group property defying a basic expression of individualism.

Correspondingly, social development, as part of the right to development, is not the same as aggregate human development; just as peace as the right of a nation in the world is not the same as peace as the sum of rights of citizens in the society. In these two examples of collective rights the problem may be that of finding individual-level equivalents rather than group-level equivalents of individual rights. However, regardless of how problematic this correspondence may be the fact is that the human condition has not only an individual but also a group mode, both surrounded by strong feelings.

Consequently, group rights will always be on the agenda: not only those that have no individual right homologue, but also others, whenever it makes a difference. It usually does.

The problem of transcendentalism   The Western formula has been to have a strong god/strong king/strong state, and compensate by strengthening the individual. Other societies, such as many tribal orders, have had neither one nor the other. Then there are the despotic orders based on strong states and weak individuals. And, of course, the fourth possibility, strong individuals inside weak states, bringing to mind such remarkable constructions as Iceland and the Faroe islands.

Many aspects of the Western formula will probably remain for a long time. But the formula can be diluted with norm-senders and norm-receivers other than states; and with norm-receivers and norm-objects other than individuals. Indeed, if we play on the full richness of *civil society* there is enough work to do, deepening and broadening the human rights tradition for generations to come.

2

HUMAN RIGHTS AND THE LEGAL TRADITION

IS THE LEGAL TRADITION STRUCTURE-BLIND?

To get more deeply into the human rights discourse we have to look at the legal tradition. To introduce that issue let us make use of a distinction between two ways of looking at human, social or for that matter world affairs: the actor-orientated and the structure-orientated perspectives.[1] They can be seen as two ways of reflecting, and reflecting on, social affairs, each of them catching something of importance, like the wave-perspective and the particle-perspective in physics. Neither of them is sufficient, but each of them is necessary. Being complementary, together they make for a relatively rich perspective. But alone they function rather like the eyes of a color-blind person, filtering out something that leaves impressions on the eyes of others, admitting something else. The metaphor is not chosen at random. There are colors involved also here: the actor-orientated perspective is more blue (conservative), the structure-orientated more red (progressive). One perspective filters out what the other perspective lets into the eyes of the beholder, making it a part of the image on which the person would act. Disturbing images are omitted; they are filtered out in advance.

And the reader will then have guessed the general thesis, in the shape of a syllogism. The legal paradigm is biased in favor of the actor-orientated perspective; that perspective has conservative bias;

the legal paradigm favors politically conservative conclusions. *Quod erat demonstrandum*? Not quite that simple. But in that general direction.

The choice of perspective is a dramatic act of commission, the non-choice of the other an equally dramatic act of omission. Each perspective taken alone constitutes a language, a discourse, an intellectual universe in which certain things can be formulated and others not, or only with great difficulty, stretching the language and the concepts so far that they no longer fit comfortably into the basic framework of the whole underlying model. If the conservative perspective is chosen we are also in a position to say something about why lawyers tend to be conservative, why radical lawyers are so few, without drawing on such trivial hypotheses as social origin in the recruitment into the profession not to mention the social destination; or the constraints put on the lawyer by the nature of the job, making present and future acts compatible with norms of the past; or the vested interests of bureaucratic or corporate employers, of state and capital. We are characterizing the perspective underlying the legal paradigm as such.

Table 2.1 gives in schematic form some of the basic properties of the two perspectives or social cosmologies. By and large the actor-orientated perspective to the left (politically to the right) is what anyone can read any day in the Western press, or most of the world press in general.[2] The basic idea is that the world is to be understood in terms of its human actors; individuals, firms, states and others (groups, organizations; domestic or global). As there are very many of them, particularly of the former, some selection has to be made in the perception process. The selection is in favor of the active and the strong. By definition they are easily discovered, making the top of the social pyramid particularly visible, with the rest of the population turning into an amorphous mass of the passive and weak. There is, however, a principle of Chinese boxes involved here. If the eyes that see are trained on the world as a whole, the superpowers and major powers in general, heads of state and governments, etc. will be discovered first, and thinking as well as action will be in terms of them. But the eyes can also be trained on sub-units and sub-sub-units, and that is how presidents of corporations and associations, the heads of families (meaning the *pater familias*, in general) mayors and chairpersons, etc. enter the picture. The perspective is capable of dissolving that amorphous mass into distinct actors, but will always over-select the strong and active. Usually high up.

Table 2.1 The actor-orientated and structure-orientated perspectives

Dimension	Actor-orientated perspective	Structure-orientated perspective
Basic unit	*Actors* (individuals, states, others)	*Structures* (positions and relations between them)
Basic dimensions	*Intention* (good vs. evil) *Capability* (weak vs. strong) *Presence* (passive vs. active)	Repression vs. freedom Exploitation vs. equity Penetration vs. autonomy Segmentation vs. integration Fragmentation vs. solidarity Marginalization vs. participation
Problem of evil	Actors that are evil, strong, active	Structures that are repressive, exploitative, penetrating, segmenting, fragmenting, marginalizing
How to cope	Make actors good, or weak or passive	Make structures free and equitable; autonomous, integrated, solidary, participatory
Basic approach	Focus on *evil* actors; building institutions to contain actors	Focus on *wrong* structures; transforming structures through revolutions
Time cosmology	Focus on acts, i.e. on *events*	Focus on structures, i.e. on *permanents*
Forgotten factor	Structures, actor-invariant aspects; structure-blindness	Actors, structure-invariant aspects; actor-blindness

That leaves us with the choice between good actors and evil ones. The hypothesis would be an over-selection of the "evil" ones, those who have already through their acts proved that they are evil, as well as those who may be suspected of harboring evil intentions. The causes of evil are seen as resting with them, expressed in their acts or threats, or general inclination to engage in evil acts. One may speculate why there should be less focus on the good actors and the good acts. One possible explanation could be as follows: "let us at least protect ourselves against evil, and hope there will be something good in addition." This "worst case analysis" is the mentality of frightened people exposed to the hazards of nature, like a ship-wrecked crew or the first immigrants to the Americas. The opposite, more optimistic attitude would be "let us facilitate and promote the good in people, and hope there will not be too much evil."[3]

The next question is what to do with those evil actors, and the answer is necessarily threefold: converting them to better intentions; weakening them by depriving them of their capability; and/or making them more passive in general. To obtain these results institutions have to be built, all the time trying to contain the evil act, and particularly the accumulation of collectively organized evil known as internal or external wars. Family, churches and schools; fines and prisons; and marginalizing social structures pacifying large parts of the population in general, and mental hospitals in particular, would belong to the repertory. The control system uses high-status people: the priest, the lawyer, the doctor; pillars of the society.

Within this framework of thinking the evil act is an *event*. It is not a state of affairs, a *Zustand*, something that was, is, and probably will continue to be. Nor is it a slowly or quickly changing state of affairs; a process. On the contrary, it is a discontinuous jump, something that is now but was different a moment ago, and may well be different thereafter. Thus, I am standing on that Italian railway station with my three bags, then suddenly I have only two bags and the thief can be seen at a distance, bag firmly in hand, himself on one of those small, highly efficient motorbikes. Or: there was "peace," then suddenly there is "war." This "jump" is what has to be prevented.

Of course, in real life there is the possibility of a continuum between the slow process and the quantum jump: the steep curve.[4] But if we should characterize this perspective, not politically (this will be done later) but from a purely perceptual point of view, one might argue that the perspective is somewhat primitive, as taken out of an early stage of cognitive development. It focuses on concrete entities, such as individuals, and appoints them the key building blocks of social reality – using social stratification (active, strong) and simple threat-perception (evil) as filtering mechanisms for selecting actors who merit particular attention. Further, it focuses on sudden, easily perceived, changes in the state of affairs of these individuals, building on the contrast effect between what was and what is. The perspective captures very well a change of property, something "mine" or "ours" that suddenly becomes "yours," "his," "hers," "theirs"; or a sudden, violent death from a brick thrown, or a shot fired, in anger. But it does not capture well a permanent state of repression, or the slow transfer of wealth known as exploitation, or the slow death known as starvation.

There is something almost infantile in the actor-orientated perspective. In this there is also strength, however: in its simplistic concreteness lies a protection against excessive concept- and theory-formation. True, there are also abstractions as when collective actors and "juridical persons," e.g. corporations and states, are introduced. But the perspective is good at capturing concrete actors, or at equipping them with concreteness by stipulating that a state should be a territorially contiguous unit with recognizable and recognized borders, with a power center capable of exercising internal control (so that others would know exactly which actors can serve as addressees of letters, or bullets).

Let us then turn to the structure-orientated perspective. This is not the place to discuss the usages of the six word-pairs suggested as basic vocabulary in a *structural* discourse; that has been done elsewhere.[5] Clearly, in this perspective such phenomena as repression (political) and exploitation (economic) in the first two dimensions, the supporting structures (the next four) and imperialism (all six combined) all become *fassbar*, to use that excellent German word, because the structural language has been built exactly for that purpose. This perspective catches types of evil, if one assumes that material or non-material repression and impoverishment, even to the point of spiritual or somatic death, are "evils," but *without presupposing evil actors*.

Thus, an imperialistic structure[6] can have disastrous consequences and yet there is not necessarily any evil intention anywhere. Obviously there are actors around, otherwise the structure would not operate. But only a segment of an actor is in any one particular structure and only a small part of a structure shows up in any one particular actor. Moreover, those actors that are particularly visible may not be particularly active, and vice versa. In fact, the actors may only be "doing their jobs." It is millions, billions, of such acts of "doing their jobs," patterned in a certain way, that add up to, or constitute, a structure, for instance an imperialist structure. So, if harm is being done unto somebody, where is the evil actor on whom to focus, to capture, arraign in court, indict, convict, and punish? Where is that particular event that should trigger institutions into action? Answer: nowhere, nowhen (at no time). Nothing outstanding stands out. All is "business as usual," even literally speaking.

Thus, aspects of the human condition that cannot be easily captured in one perspective can be captured in the other; suggesting that the two perspectives are complementary. Taken alone both of them are too one-sided. One sees evil in terms of sudden events, the evil act of the evil actor, and suggests as a remedy something permanent, an institution with a social structure with controllers on top and the controlled at the bottom. The other sees evil in terms of something permanent, the permanent wrong wrought by the false structure, and suggests as remedy a sudden event, a revolution (violent or non-violent) brought about by good, strong, and active actors. Each perspective has to invoke the other to remedy evil.

One perspective tends to be structure-blind. But the other tends to be actor-blind, in the sense of being insensitive to the peculiarities of actors, categorizing them merely as "bourgeois," "proletariat" or as "center" vs. "periphery," etc. Our contention is certainly not that one is wrong and the other right, but that each of them is incomplete, without for that reason claiming that their combination would be "complete." Thus, as described here they are both too weak on the dimension of time, process and too undialectical. The sum of two color-blind visions is not necessarily full or "normal" vision; nor does the sum of two color-blind social perspectives add up to the full truth and nothing but the truth. But eclecticism helps.

Let us then try to characterize the legal perspective, although what follows may have the vices and virtues of the caricature to some, and of important insight to others. No doubt it is exaggerated, and it applies better to criminal law than to civil law and process law. Something will be said about that later.

We shall assume that the basic constituent of the legal perspective is the "juridical person," an actor, as something to which legal norms may apply. They are norm-receivers in the sense of being capable of receiving norms. Some of them may also be norm-senders in the sense of being capable of sending norms. The juridical person may be an individual or collective actor; in the latter case some individuals within the collectivity usually have specific tasks to perform in a legal context. In the former case there are some limitations ruling out some individuals as juridical persons (children, the mentally ill; sometimes categories defined in terms of gender, race, class, nation, etc.).

Characteristic of juridical persons is that they are equipped with intentions and capabilities, and hence with responsibilities. *Structures cannot be juridical persons* with intentions and capabilities. They cannot distinguish between right and wrong according to legal standards classifying action as right/indifferent/wrong built into the laws/treaties that have been ratified by appropriate bodies. It is not enough that others classify behavior; the actor must also be capable of doing so. If the conclusion is "wrong," the actor should abstain from the act, risk bad conscience, or risk others applying normative standards. There then follows the legal routine, leading to apprehension and adjudication, possibly verifying that conclusion, convicting the actor, and then imposing sanctions with a view to obtaining non-evil behavior in the future from the same actor (individual prevention) or other actors (general prevention) to whom the same norms would apply. Usually there is also the possibility of appeal, and some validation of the entire process by an appropriate competent authority.[7] If not in fact, at least in theory: a juridical person is an actor capable of being both receiver (to himself or herself) of the relevant norms. Only the actor knows what is expected of him or her and can expect of himself or herself the "right" behavior. An animal, a tree, a celestial body, or a structure may be the source of evil but cannot be norm-sender and/or norm-receiver. Or so we assume, under the rules of modernity.

The actor-orientated perspective shows up in a number of places in this legalistic paradigm.

First, as already pointed out: the basic unit is an actor equipped with at least the capacity for having intentions and capabilities and for being active; meaning enacting them, in an evil way, thereby infracting norms properly arrived at.

Second, the legal perspective tries to use the three methods under "how to cope with it":

1   making actors *good* by exposing them to the normative expectations through family, church and school;

2   making actors *weak* by punishing them – depriving them of free
    time or free money (or more bodily forms of incapacitating
    punishment, ultimately including execution);
3   making actors *passive* by locking them in or out (expelling them)
    or otherwise (lobotomy, ataraxia, etc.) deterring them from any
    evil-doing.

However, there is actually very little, if any at all, emphasis on
making actors "good," not only "non-evil," by converting them.
Operating within the same discourse there would be considerable
affinities between the two activities. But the latter is left to another
actor-orientated institution, the church. The legal system is very
poor in terms of positive approaches, but not as a consequence of its
actor-orientation, that perspective opens for rewards as well as
punishment. Religions like Christianity are more effective in this
regard by being more symmetrical, showing both what is right and
what is wrong; trying to instill a desire for the former and distaste for
the latter; encouraging the good-doer through promises of eternal
rewards, discouraging the evil-doer into at least passivity through
threats of eternal punishment. Christianity and Islam have both
Heaven and Hell in their repertory; the legal profession only a
secular version of the latter. But both of them have concrete actors
as their subjects, with the important difference that Christianity
tends to focus on individual to the neglect of the collective actors.
And neither of them can handle structures (not the same as
collectivities, incidentally).

Third, it is important if not absolutely essential that the evil act is
intended. There is such a thing as negligence, acts of omission. But
that very concept indicates the weight attributed to the dimension of
intention. Lack of intention, moreover, does not necessarily mean
consciouslessness. It could also be interpreted to mean that there is
an intention but in another direction, such as the soldier who kills;
not with the intention of harming anybody, but with the intention of
revenging his buddies, defending himself, his country, freedom, the
revolution. In other words, there has to be some kind of coincidence
between subjective intention and objective harm for certificates of
guilt to be distributed in the adjudication process. Unobtainable for
structures.

Fourth, not only is the perspective actor-orientated, it is also what
one might call negatively structure-orientated. Thus, if an actor

commits an act that can be seen as "normal" in the precise sense that other actors in the same position commit the same acts in the same situation; in other words, *if the evil act is actor-invariant*, it is not captured in this particular grid. One husband who beats his wife excessively may be detected, reported, evaluated, convicted, punished; one billion husbands who exploit one billion wives in an institution called marriage, in a patriarchy, are left undetected, unreported, etc. One soldier who commits a My Lai massacre is punished; half a million who engage directly or indirectly in less explicit massacres pass unpunished. The willingness to punish the unusual, not entirely actor-invariant, can also be seen as a risk that has to be assumed by those who have a vested interest in the structure. Needless to say, they will generally be the people on top of the structure, domestic or global, and prefer paradigms, images and conceptual frameworks in general that locate "evil" in the unusual and the actor-specific, not in the normal and the actor-invariant built into the everyday working of the structure.

What about the actor who commits evil acts regardless of structural context – in other words, *the evil actor whose evil is structure-invariant*? The perennial bully, what about him? The approach is different. That particular person is not declared guilty of evil acts, but declared sick, mentally insane as proved by the fact that he cannot function normally in any context. In other words, the condition for issuing a certificate of evilness is not only that the actor engages in unusual and harmful behavior in *some* context, but that the evil act can be seen as the outcome of a conscious deliberate choice, as proved by the circumstance that in *other* contexts (or, in the same context but in earlier periods) such acts are/were not committed. Thus, the legal paradigm is in a sense setting up two filters: one against the structure-invariant evil actor, the other against the actor-invariant evil structure. Neither of them is captured by the paradigm.

At this point one might ask: why should they? Why should the legal paradigm be capable of catching everything evil in this world? Would that not be an even greater danger, the all-pervasive thought-form, capable of coming to grips with all evils between heaven and earth? Even above the skies into paradise, and below the earth into the other place?

This is a valid point. We are not in search of a general theory of evil, complete with all possible mechanisms for its eradication. There have been such efforts in human history and they tend to legitimize very powerful elites, who in the name of the eradication of evil commit evils at least commensurate with those they are supposed to eradicate; compare the Inquisition in Catholic Europe, the witch-burning in Protestant Europe, the extermination processes in Nazi Germany and the Stalinist Soviet Union.

But there is another argument in this connection. Thus, to the extent that law is compatible with one paradigm rather than another, and the paradigms or perspectives themselves are parts of a political reality favoring some rather than other views and groups and parties, *law becomes politics*. As an intellectual game this is innocuous. But as a forceful culture, legitimizing some and delegitimizing other social and world relations, it is far from innocuous. Thus, it is far from innocuous that within the legal paradigm UN definition of military aggression comes easily and the definition of "economic aggression" not, to the point that quotation marks have to be introduced for the latter. Why? Because military aggression satisfies all the characteristics built into the actor-orientated perspective: it is made by actors who have to be "evil" from the point of view of the victim and are "strong" or at least believe themselves so as proved by the concrete act of transgression, e.g. a sudden invasion, bombing an open city, firing the first shot not in defense against somebody else firing a first shot. Compare this to economic aggression that just *is*. There is vertical division of labor, exploitation in other words; the periphery is penetrated by the center, conditioned, caused by it; the periphery participates with a small segment of its potential, the center fully; the total structure fragments the periphery and unites the centers; and the structure draws a line between the first (center) and the second (periphery) class participants in the system marginalizing the latter; whether the system is a factory, a firm, or an international economic system.

To take but one aspect of this: it is easy to see who should be apprehended, arraigned into court, adjudicated, and eventually punished if an act of military aggression is performed. If the system is not capable of inflicting any punishment it may at least aim at deterrence through balance of power policies or simple revanche/ revenge in lieu of that. Except for the difficulty in finding the initial act in an *actio-reactio* chain of provocations and counter-provocations disguised as defensive responses, there may be something somewhere that fits the actor-orientated model; e.g. by choosing a time zero (Pearl Harbor, Iraq's occupation of Kuwait), limiting geographical and social space to zoom in on evil.

Not so with economic aggression. The first step may be so imperceptible and in addition not easily classified as "evil." A country or a firm makes a small investment in the form of a governmental or non-governmental development assistance project with the best intentions. However, after some time the imperialist structure is there, in full bloom. Who is guilty? Can a structure be arrested and arraigned in court? Can a structure be made to confess its sins, atoning for them? Not so easy, for the simple reason that the structure is not a juridical person but something abstract, something one cannot easily draw a line around, and say *eccolo*!

The latter, however, is no longer so true as it used to be. With the advent of the transnational corporation (TNC), bringing together capital, technology and management, there is more organizational coherence than there used to be between structures and actors. In the transnational corporation the five structurally negative properties referred to above as characteristics of a wrong economic structure (others may have other dimensions and definitions) are built into the corporation. The corporation is an incorporated actor, having a center of control with a "mind" capable of formulating goals and devising strategies to obtain them. Within the TNC the general imperialist structure is replicated, only that the "countries" have become "corporations." The center–periphery idea is expressed softly in family, even female terms: mother vs. daughter (companies). The rest is the same, with the managers of the "daughter" companies being the center in the periphery of this conveyor belt of production factors and products, administrative decisions, and research findings.

By incorporating the structures as transnational corporations they are making themselves more compatible with the legal paradigm. The structures have become actors. The debate is over the extent to which they are accountable, and how they can shift everything around so that profits show up (if at all) only in places where there is a "climate friendly to business." Labor-intensive work is carried out in places where labor is cheap, fragmented, and marginalized and hence less able to defend itself and fight for its interests. This is an important debate; and no solution transcending that problem is in sight.

Even more important is the debate over how one can identify non-incorporated structures. Thus, as soon as a code of conduct for TNCs is established the TNCs may transform themselves so as to comply, and leave the less palatable aspects to the non-incorporated, more fragmented, parts of the total world economic structure. Again, the argument would be that law might be mystifying, providing a pretense that something is being done to a problem while in reality brushing it under the carpet. And the carpet is provided by a legal pattern transforming some parts of the structure in a way which is *fassbar* by the paradigm, while at the same time concealing the total structure.

Again, this is not an argument against law or lawyers as such; but a critique of the legal paradigm in so far as it contributes to a mystification of social reality because people start believing that it constitutes a generally valid approach to all aspects of social life. That it does not is obvious to many. For instance, most people would understand that laws are not good at catching a process, but better at coming to grips with existing states of affairs and a clearly defined set of actors. Dynamism is easily seen as deviance. By this we do not merely think of the obvious, that social life is ever-changing whereas the institutions for changing laws grind out new laws slowly. Occasionally laws may be leading. But they tend to be lagging behind the social reality they are supposed not only to reflect (that is the task of social science), but to regulate, which invariably means stabilizing, freezing social processes at some point.

We are thinking more of the circumstance that laws tend not to build dynamism and dialectics into their visions. They depict and regulate a *state of affairs* where certain acts are proscribed. The rest is left open. The focus on the evil acts leaves a lot of free play for the indifferent acts and for the good acts, the deeds – but there is nevertheless something frozen about the image given. And it is difficult to conceive of it differently: a "dynamic" law indicating that what is forbidden today may be permitted after 1 January next year relativizes right and wrong and confuses not only the evil-doer. On the other hand, this difficulty in imagining a dynamic legal system may also be a sign of how "brain-washed" we have become by the present paradigm, so poor in reasoning along the dimension of time.

What then, one might ask, would happen to this pattern of argument if one changes from the paradigm of criminal law to that of civil law as an instrument that draws a line between proscribed and permitted not to convict and punish but to build, even develop further more adequate structures? Is this not the instrument needed: a way of catching, in normative form, an image of a good social reality?

It is, and it is not. It can be to the extent that the image of the "good" social reality is informed by sufficient insight in structural aspects of society, and in social processes. But we have argued above that this insight is not facilitated by the legal paradigm simply because it one-sidedly opts in favor of the actor-orientated perspective. And this applies even more to contractual relations between collective actors because the individuals signing or entering the contract will tend to be from the top of the collective actor and the relation to the rest may be tenuous. In addition, the parties at the top, two chief executives for instance, may have a harmony of interest built into the contract that does not apply deeper down in the two social pyramids they represent. In reality, the contract unites the top and fragments the bottom. The term "collective actor" applies to the elites rather than to what they represent. Thus it is that contracts or treaties easily become "scraps of paper": they are intra-elite contracts not reflecting the structures in which these elites are embedded. Signatures and elite agreements are too weak and too biased as instruments of social cohesion. A guerrilla leader who enters into an agreement with the oppressor to secure independence on certain conditions may be accused by the movement to change the structure of having committed a sell-out and be deposed, and what is the value of his signature if he is no longer a leader?[8]

To take a more specific example: imagine a treaty drafted in the 1970s about the nodules down on the ocean floor, on the seabed.[9] Their content is metallic: manganese, nickel, cobalt, copper. Governments conclude a treaty that gives powerful, technologically developed countries (i.e. principally the United States and the former Soviet Union) the right to mine the ocean floor against payment of royalties to an international seabed authority, and to the governments of developing countries. A new inter-governmental organization, a regime, has been born. Activity starts and the following scenario is activated: nodules are mined, the metallic content is extracted, processed, and marketed and the proceeds are used to cover the costs, for reinvestment, for profit, and for royalties. These last, however, being money, flow into the empty bank accounts of Third World governments and elites rather than into the empty stomachs of Third World people. The money in those bank accounts, governmental or non-governmental, tends to be put to private or public purposes that do not necessarily benefit the people. One reason is very simple: money *can* be used for the satisfaction of basic material needs, but a capital-intensive "modern" technology is likely to generate very vertical, center–periphery–type structures,[10] and also to price the final product out of the reach of the masses.

There is no need to go into the political economics of these processes. What happens is actually very simple. The basic material-need satisfiers are such things as food, clothes, shelter, health, education. For all of them the metal content in terms of manganese, nickel, cobalt, and copper is negligible. To believe that there is a simple conversion mechanism from metal to food or education is naive. The transformations via tractors, etc. are few and often too capital-intensive, and school buildings can be made of wood and brick. Moreover, there is also the distinct possibility that the metal will be processed into "bads" (arms – the military industry has a demand structure compatible with the nodule supply structure) rather than "goods," and used to control those with empty stomachs by (threats of) direct violence, or by selling the arms to elites with vested interests in the status quo in the Third World countries.

Seen in this perspective it is not so strange if a treaty is signed, well knowing that even that is a major accomplishment. The treaty might be built around a solid harmony of interests at the elite levels: the interests of the industrialized countries in raw materials, of super-power military industries to be ahead of all others by focusing on nodules and deep sea mining out of reach for most other countries, *and* the interests of non-industrialized elites in convertible currency for whatever purpose. And those with the empty stomachs are left out of the whole process. Brushed under the carpet. Could it be that some of the same applies to human rights conventions?

The legal paradigm too easily lends itself to that kind of outcome. Of course, there are remedial mechanisms, such as composing national delegations in a more representative manner. More particu-larly, if the delegations consisted mainly of hungry and angry people the results might be different. But such people would not be *salonfähig*, and usually incapable of drafting the instruments. It is also possible that with 50 percent of the delegates being women there might have been less fascination with metals and more with food, hence less of a focus on nodules and more on sustainable ocean-farming of various kinds.

The important point is that such safeguards do not follow automatically from the paradigm; they are not built into it. The treaties negotiated are between collective actors that are states, and will reflect a balance of *national interests* rather than the "lower level" actors and their interests, *human needs*. The perspective is not only silent on the structure between actors; it is also silent on the structure within actors, preserving and promoting the billiard ball image of collective actors in general and national actors in particular.

The conclusion will have to be a justified skepticism rather than any all-out war on legal thinking. There are those who have used law very well for purposes serving the progress of humankind. But the basic paradigm is too one-sided, too biased, too ideological. Time has come for a basic change, not only for clever intra-paradigmatic maneuvers. Such tasks may not be carried out by international law commissions. Possibly some of the new forces emerging in the world can lay the ground for a new paradigm combining the actor- and structure-orientated perspectives, promoting an international law that would be human law, not stopping at the gates of the state, but bridging the gap between collective and individual actors better than is done today. As usual the key condition for change is consciousness, and more sensitivity to the actor–structure relationship.[11]

IS THE LEGAL TRADITION CULTURE-BLIND?

Having explored the difficulties in coming to grips with social and world structures, the problem to be explored in this section is the relationship between the legal tradition and cultural diversity. The focus is not on whether a single legal tradition can work equally well in different cultures; it obviously cannot, as was pointed out in chapter 1. The focus is on how different cultures shape the legal tradition in general and the operation of the general legal paradigm of norms(laws)–infraction–detection–adjudication–sentence–sanctions.

Let me start with a dramatic example. A nation as law-abiding and rule-orientated as the Germans, with laws and rules so deeply embedded in their culture, became a Nazi state with 110,000 people in the SS, SA and SD exterminating 11 million human beings, 6 million of them Jews, and with as many as 7 million people being members of the Nazi party.[12]

The problem to be explored can be stated as follows. On the one hand there are the Nazi crimes and horrors. Some highly concrete humans had to commit those horrendous crimes – and not only the 110,000; also the many who worked in the infrastructure making it possible, such as the famous railroaders, more or less knowing what they did. On the other hand, there is the German inclination not only to use words, but to use strong and very explicit words, *Gebete*, *Gebote*, *Gesetze*, to convey explicit, universal norms of conduct. Think of Luther, of Kant; for instance, of the moral injunction *"Handle immer so, dass die Maxime deines Willens als eine allgemeine Gesetzgebung gelten könnte,"* with the focus on the word (*"Maxime"*) rather than the consequences. And of the general inclination towards axiomatic, deductive thinking, with much *zurückführen* and *ableiten*.[13]

The German problem was, and remains: why did not all these commandments, principles, laws, norms, and values, and all these Germans who had recited all these words and internalized them, not stem the tide toward Nazism? Centuries of Christianity in general, and Lutheran Christianity in particular, with words, orally and in writing, millions, billions of them, poured over generations of Germans, should that not have had a deterrent effect with all those promises of bad conscience and punishment in this life or thereafter? True, *exterminism* is also found in the Old and New Testaments as something a revengeful God legitimately engages in, and rightly so according to his representative on earth, Jesus Christ.[14] But in the Bible this prerogative was reserved for God (and the Son) and not extended to the lesser creatures of his creation. In principle, Christianity should stand in the way of Nazism, and so should the equally actor-orientated legal tradition to a large extent derived from it.

Instead the system produced the most flagrant contradiction between norms and behavior, between values and facts.[15] The question then becomes: how are contradictions between verbally formulated norms and behavior handled? In general this depends on the relative strength of the two. If the norms are very strong, in the sense of being internalized (conscience) and/or institutionalized (reward/punishment), they will win out and behavior dissonant with them will be met with negative sanctions; bad conscience and/or punishment. Religion and law are built around these textbook mechanisms. More particularly, the first line of defense of the social order embedded in the norms is internalization, the second is institutionalization. Obviously, both broke down in Nazi Germany, if they were ever there.

What happens if the deviant behavior is so grossly dissonant, and engaged in by so many that it is obvious to everybody that the negative sanctions do not "bite?" What to do in that case? Change the behavior, change the norms, both or neither? And for all four cases, how is that done? This very question will be used as a handle on the general problem of the relationship between the legal tradition and the underlying culture. The basic thesis is this: legal traditions differ precisely in how they, explicitly or implicitly, answer this question. One way of answering the question is by defining the deviant case as so special that the norms do not apply. This was the approach chosen in the case of Nazi Germany for the great majority of those directly or indirectly engaged in the crimes, as will be indicated later. But there are other approaches, such as the Anglo-Saxon (common law), Roman and Japanese approaches.

The Anglo-Saxon (and Nordic) approach would be to regard *a (set of) norm(s) as a (set of) prediction(s)*, to be tested against empirical reality, much in the same way descriptive hypotheses are tested. If there is, *grosso modo*, consonance between behavioral norms and behavioral facts, then the norms have stood the test. But if the cases of dissonance are too far from the norm, too many, or too tenacious, then the norms have to be handled like hypotheses in the empirical sciences. They have to be adjusted to behavior to make the normative order work better as a prediction of social reality.[16] As in empirical science those who insist that norms rather than behavior have to be changed must then come up with alternative norms (hypotheses) that can predict and legitimize better the new behavior. The legal system defends itself against irrelevance through flexibility.

This is, of course, similar to the scientific procedure in general, with one rather important difference. It is not the depersonalized objects natural sciences have constructed out of nature that stand up, rebelling against scientific hypotheses, but people themselves who stand up against norms not only prescribing but also predicting their behavior to make the social order look more orderly. An obvious example would be the ongoing transformation of sexual mores. Tactical retreat makes sense if moral authority is measured by consonance.

But before a tactical retreat the law-makers will have to reflect on the basic question in the Roman (and also Germanic) approach: can the norm(s) be changed without doing basic harm to the entire normative construction, or are they so firmly anchored deductively in the core of that construction that a removal would do harm to the entire edifice? This problem of deductive coherence (as opposed to the empirical consonance problem mentioned above) has its obvious homologue in theory construction in the empirical sciences. A scientist may easily revise a peripheral prediction. But a thesis central to the whole construction will be defended and dissonances will be seen as special cases, observation errors, etc.[17]

For the predictive element in a prescription to take the upper hand, behavior (facts) has to be given more weight than morals (norms). Not only data/norms about people but people themselves have to be taken seriously. People report through deeds and/or words that this or that norm does not make sense and may have to be revised. If channels of communication are open there may even be a dialogue, a *communitas* between norm-sender and norm-receiver.

However, norm-senders may insist on the sacredness of some norms to prolong the life expectancy for the total normative construction. This theological/philosophical position may be protected socially through heterogeneity and inequality; the norm-senders belonging to another and higher class. Tenacious evidence from the norm-objects to the effect that neither internalization nor institutionalization works in no way invalidates the construction. In that case the good Anglo-Saxon/Nordic citizen is no longer the person who conforms with the norms (or conceals his or her deviance), but one who makes that deviance a matter of principle, assuming the consequences of his or her civil disobedience, and then participates in the dialogue of deeds and words about normative reconstruction. No wonder the civil disobedience tradition (Thoreau, Gandhi) is linked to Anglo-Saxon law: the assumption being that not only can law invalidate behavior; under some circumstances behavior can also invalidate law.[18]

The opposite case, homogeneity/equality without willingness to revise verbal constructions, is also possible. In the Latin countries of southern Europe and South America there is considerably less willingness to change the normative construction. One may perhaps add norms, but not subtract or change, even when heterogeneity and inequality (class) should not stand in the way. The written word is seen as more sacred than in the Anglo-Saxon/Nordic cultures, and not only to maintain the deductive structure unmolested. The verbal construction becomes an end in itself. Much work is invested in making the oral presentation euphonic, pleasant to listen to; and the written presentation aesthetic, nice to look at.

Thus, there is no coincidence between general willingness to revise a prescriptive framework and such social factors as homogeneity and equality. We may have one without the other. The slaves in the US slave states were not part of any *communitas* with their rulers, but were forced to adjust to the norms/roles governing their behavior, not vice versa. And yet they and the abolitionists somehow won, by behaving as if the slaves were free. And the norms were adjusted accordingly. The same holds for women, children, foreigners, animals.

But then the words can also be detached from reality and become a very poor guide, for norm-senders and norm-receivers alike, to a reality much less perfect than a well-crafted and drafted verbal construction. The words take on a life of their own. It is incorrect, as many outsiders assert, that Latins will tend to think that a problem is solved once it is solved rhetorically, or on paper. The difference between Latins and others is not that words are seen as the solution to the real problem, but that the verbal solution is important in its own right, with all the socio-cultural connotations that carries, among other reasons because of the pleasure derived from good craftsmanship, and the prestige derived from being a master in the field. In the stratum of words, that is.

How, then, can one handle deviant behavior if the norms are unchangeable and the sanctions do not work/are too costly? Perhaps essentially by accepting that the deviance is against the legal but not against the statistical norm. The law-breaker may *confess*, in the religious tradition, that deviant behavior has been engaged in, showing due, i.e. verbal, respect for the word. If somebody does something "wrong," but confesses, punitive sanctions deposited in the verbal stratum may not have to be administered beyond verbal rebukes. A two-tiered structure has been established, the theological/legal construction of an ideal world reflected in ideal words (commandments and laws, confessions and rebukes), and the real world of behavioral infractions and sanctions. A world of words; a world of facts. Even gross dissonance is insufficient reason for revisions of key theological/legal constructions. Beautiful words reflect an ideal world, not to be taken as a model of the real one.[19]

Japanese normative culture might represent a third possible approach. Given the vagueness built into the language Japanese statements easily render themselves open to interpretations. Consequently, cases of dissonance can be handled by interpreting the norms, and/or statements about the facts, stretching them conceptually. This should not be seen as a trick, or as ambiguity built into normative language on purpose in order to guard against excessive dissonance in the future, but as a basic characteristic of Japanese culture. The question, of course, is *who* is permitted to interpret. Norm-senders and norm-receivers may together constitute an interpretation *communitas*, but a very vertical one with the senders on top. Any statement is seen as more, not less, valid if it can harbor more meanings than one, possibly because the world is seen as so fluid and ambiguous that nothing single-valued, only the verbally ambiguous, can serve as a mirror. It is through vagueness rather than precision that a verbal model becomes adequate.[20]

Thus, the general thesis so far is that the Anglo-Saxons/Nordics would tend to save the normative culture by changing it, being essentially flexible, case-orientated, experimental in their attitude. The Latins would tend to save the normative culture by retaining it and embellishing it, giving it the status of a piece of culture rather than a really prescriptive, not to mention predictive, not to mention descriptive, guide to behavior. The Japanese would tend to save the normative culture by stretching it so that it covers a broader range of behavior, finding a "solution" not so much by introducing new laws (Anglo-Saxon), or invoking common (Catholic priest) sense and personal relations (Latin case), as by reinterpreting the norms, claiming that the new norm was already there. The question is: what did the Germans do?

On the one hand, there are the impressive German normative and legal systems/pyramids, constructed like Teutonic thought pyramids in general. On the other hand, there is the real world of real people; in struggle and cooperation, in hatred and love. As mentioned, the two worlds can clash and major problems of dissonance can arise. But the three solutions mentioned above are all ruled out, for different reasons. The Anglo-Saxon solution presupposes a detached attitude to normative constructions, viewing them as transitory. The Germans may know that their constructions are not permanent, but nevertheless relate to them as if they were. Hence there is less willingness to change the rules. Quite a lot of work went into making them, probably more than in most other cultures, and with more deductive talent, more *"zurückführen/ableiten."* The Latin solution coincides with the German solution in regarding the norms as rather sacred, as being made if not for eternity at least for a very long period, and for some of the same reasons. But the Germans would be less willing to see norms as ideal, detached from reality. They would tend to see norms as even more real than reality, and to see reality as an imperfect reflection of the norms, rather than seeing the normative system as an imperfect guide to reality. To give common sense "the upper hand" is to give in to anarchy. This means that norms cannot be changed; ideally they should remain valid come what may. That should lead to the Japanese solution. But this is not available in the Germanic culture either, the language being far too precise and much too much work having been invested into producing exactly that unambiguity.

Consequently, the Germans are in a relatively tough situation: they cannot easily change the rules, they cannot easily detach them from empirical reality, they cannot easily reinterpret them. So, what does one do in the case when (a) behavior totally contrary to the rules is massively engaged in and cannot be stopped and/or (b) such behavior is even encouraged? Returning to that historical problem: how could the Nazi crimes initiated in February 1933 be tolerated, given the whole weight of German moralism and legalism, of German Christianity and fastidious state construction combined? One key is given by the frequent references in 1983, during the fiftieth anniversary, to the "brown hordes." Nazis were often referred to as "brutes." The conclusion drawn by many Germans from that premise is elegant as a solution, but at the same time highly problematic: the norms did not apply.

The normative framework, however much an embodiment, a purified version of reality, simply did not apply to the Nazi phenomena because these people were no longer humans. That way the normative framework could escape intact from the sharp encounter with reality. Get rid of the brutes (party bosses and SS people) and underneath is an unmolested society. The victims, the communists in Kreuzberg, the social democrats in Schöneberg (and Köpenick) and the Jews all over, did not draw that conclusion. They certainly saw themselves as humans, and the Nazis as brutal, fascist, but also as humans, accountable to the law, and to whom the laws should have been applied. But more important than the victims was the German *Bürgerschaft*, the people of Charlottenburg/Dahlem/ Grünewald, to put it in Berlin terms. By restricting applicability *the normative construction was saved because it did not apply*. This was an *Ausnahmezustand*, a *sui generis*, like fighting among animals. It was the *blonde Bestie* at work and only that. Normal norms were locked out, they were for normal times.

But even if the SA were seen as brown hordes, beyond legal norms, how could so many Germans also see people on the left as somebody to whom moral norms did not apply, meaning that they did not have to come to their rescue? The answer is probably very simple: they were seen as "extremist." Jewish friends and close colleagues may not have been seen in that vein. But if able to conjure on their inner eye images of concentration camps, gas, and ovens they were probably filled with visions of sub-humans, hungry, dirty, emaciated skeletons, not of normal-looking friends and colleagues. They became the easy victims of exactly what the Nazis intended: treat individuals as though they are sub-human, in a concentration camp, and they turn out not only to look, but also to behave as sub-humans, relative to food, relative to one another. And most importantly: they will be regarded by others as sub-human. The normative model was saved by not being applied. *Grundsätzlich*, basically, thou shalt not kill, and certainly not exterminate. But this case was simply different; the brute had broken out of the human shell, fighting the sub-humans.

In short, the hypothesis is that the phenomenon was set apart, bracketed, so that standard normative systems no longer applied. If not legitimized Nazism was at least not forbidden. Important in this connection, and the Nazis might not agree, would be the idea that the Nazis were included in this phenomenon to be set apart. And that makes the mechanism even more dangerous because it also dehumanized the Nazis, depriving them of their right and duty to be responsible for their acts. Many Nazis who surfaced in Western Germany even at the top of the republic seem to have been pardoned by this formula because "everybody is a little wild in his youth."

So the conclusion is that the normative construction did not stand in the way of Nazism; not because it was so weak, but because it was so strongly worded and constructed that it became inapplicable. If it had been applied it would have been broken. Rather than being changed; put aside. Nazism produced its own rules on the side; *Führerbefehle*, for instance. The training of the German population, through Lutheranism in general and the teaching of *zwei Regimenten* in particular, must have played an important role in accepting a division of social reality into two parts with relatively non-overlapping normative systems.[21]

According to this perspective there is a basic similarity between the legal traditions and the ideal-type intellectual styles of the four cultures, the "Saxonic," "Teutonic," "Gallic," and "Nipponic" styles.[22] To wit:

1   The Anglo-Saxon/Nordic normative culture would be compatible with the Saxonic intellectual style: low emphasis on deductive rigor, much on correspondence with the world of facts. Norms that do not fit may be discarded. New norms are *substituted*.

2   The German normative culture would be compatible with Teutonic intellectual style: high emphasis on deductive rigor, less on correspondence with facts. Facts that do not fit are made invisible. The old pyramid is not rejected. New norms may be *added*.

3   The Latin normative culture would be compatible with the Gallic intellectual style: high emphasis on verbal elegance rather than deductive rigor, less on correspondence with the world of facts. Facts that do not fit are treated on a case-by-case basis. The normative system is for admiration more than adherence. Norms are *preserved*.

4   The Japanese normative culture would be compatible with the Nipponic normative culture: low emphasis on deductive rigor, much on correspondence with the world of facts. But this can be obtained through skilful reinterpretation rather than the other means mentioned. Norms are *interpreted*.

But how could it be different? Lawyers and law-makers are intellectuals coming out of the same cultures and social classes; often even from the same families. Some become lawyers, some choose other intellectual pursuits. We are entitled to expect a certain consistency and coherence between intellectual styles in general and the different legal traditions in particular.[23]

There are some important implications to be drawn, with care, from this exercise.

The first and strong formulation would be: just as there are no universal laws in the scientific sense there are no universal laws in the legal sense. This is not so because the phenomena reflected in descriptive and prescriptive laws are too complex or too diverse, but because "law" means very different things to different cultures. This also applies to systems of laws, in other words to *science* as the whole body of descriptive/systematic construction of reality and to *law* as the whole body of prescriptive/systematic construction of social reality. It applies to the single proposition, descriptive or prescriptive, and to the systems of such propositions. The cultural differences are social realities. And that leads to the second, weaker formulation: just as there is no universal science, there is no universal law.

Except, that is, if the West in its present mainstream form were able to impose upon the rest of the world its particular atomistic/deductive epistemology. But the further that trend continues the stronger the counter-trends, unless we assume that human and social dialectics, i.e. history, has come to an end. And that would be a rather far-fetched assumption. A more reasonable assumption would be that present Western mainstream hegemony will come to an end, sooner or later. And that subjugated legal traditions will emerge.

COMPLEMENTING THE LEGAL TRADITION: NEEDS, STRUCTURE, PROCESS

The conclusion from the two preceding sections can only be that law in general, and human rights in particular, cannot be left to the legal tradition alone. It is too important to be a monopoly of a tradition so unable to react adequately to social evils built into the social structures at the social and/or world levels, while at the same time harboring pretensions of a cultural universalism that does not hold up in practice.

One problem with the latter would be that infractions of human rights are evaluated and adjudicated according to Anglo-Saxon/Nordic standards, also when these may not be the standards of the local culture. German normative culture, according to the theory expounded in the preceding section, may use the "special case" logic; Latin normative culture may regard the human rights tradition as beautiful, but perhaps too beautiful for this world; and Japanese normative culture may start interpreting, making use of the richness of the Japanese language, and more particularly of the oral homonyms covered by the same written ideograms. A false consensus emerges if lawyers who have internalized Anglo-Saxon normative culture communicate better with colleagues than with their own people. And another problem is the difficulty with group rights in a highly individualistic Western culture.

And the basic problem with the former is, of course, that only a fraction of the problems the human rights tradition tries to address can be adequately conceived of, or even addressed, within an actor-orientated discourse. Chapter 4 will elaborate that proposition in some detail with regard to three major concerns of humankind in general and the UN in particular: various aspects of development, environment, and peace.[24]

There are solid factors behind these two problems: "deep structure," and "deep culture." But even if they are intractable, difficult to change, we can at least get a conceptual handle on them. Thus, a structure is *patterned interaction*, with each act performed approximately the same way by actors in the same situation (sociologists would say "status"). Two sayings often accompany such acts: "everybody does it that way," and "we always did it that way," testifying to synchronous and diachronous constancy, hence normalcy. But what everybody does nobody does[25] in the sense of really doing it, like *res communis* = *res nullius* (what everybody owns nobody owns).[26] "Deep structure" is abstracted from this, dropping "approximately."

A "deep culture" is a socio-cultural code embedded in the collective subconscious, defining for that collectivity (e.g. a civilization) what is normal/natural.[27] Being subconscious there is no individual awareness of the deeply rooted cultural standards steering everybody, the result of the most extensive brainwashing in the world: raising children. Being collective it is shared, meaning that the individual is surrounded by others with the same assumptions. The contrast would come through deep encounters[28] with others coded differently; a deep learning experience if the threat perception is overcome. If a deep structure is rooted in the deep culture, which it almost has to be, then we are running up against something very solid indeed. The relevant example here would be a deep culture defining individuals as real and society only as a set, not as a structure of individuals. Knots, not nets. As a consequence a structure, here called "the legal tradition," emerges.

But first an elaboration of the cultural example hinted at above: the difficulty the (Western) human rights tradition has coming to grips with group rights in general, and peoples' rights in particular. As has been argued in chapter 1, a group is a set of individuals, a human group is a set of human individuals, and if group human rights can be realized as sets of individual human rights then there is no problem. The problem arises when they differ. Examples would include groups that argue rights not only to education but to their own style of education, not only to health but to their own style of health, not only to property but to collective property (and this is a very sticky point!), not only to individual, autonomous self-determination but to collective, autonomous self-determination. Combining the last two points, assuming national territory as collective property to be the group/people-level homologue of individual land as private property, the right to self-determination as usually conceived of emerges. Since this is also a group right why has this one been accepted and other group rights not?

One answer may be found in the US model of a group right: the Declaration of Independence, 1776.[29] Arguments against the right to national self-determination because it is a group right would be arguments against the birth certificate of the US, and with that of most other countries in the world that have argued independence. On the other hand, to accept national self-determination but not other group human rights, including national rights for less than self-determination, is illogical. And it may also be counterproductive for those who use this argument to favor status quo, preferring fragmentation of a minority into individuals with separate rights even when these rights are not separable. If self-determination is accepted and other group rights not, why not go all the way, using *actio popularis* even when none was intended, and less was demanded? Why create a false dichotomy between group and individual rights when the answer may be a both–and rather than an either–or, often with group rights being a condition for realizing individual rights?

Groups and peoples are then seen, essentially, as sets of individuals. "States" are different. They are organizations within territories referred to as "countries," with such sub-organizations as legislature, executive and judiciary. States are not sets of individuals in the sense of citizens; societies are.

Consequently, rights of states in the interstate system are at least two steps, not only one, removed from the human rights of individuals. What accrues to states according to some right may also end precisely there, with the members of the state as organization, as when improving the health of a country is interpreted as improving the physical facilities of the Ministry of Health and the health situation of its officials. Positive effects may accrue to the citizens, but also may not. The Charter of Rights and Duties of States (CERDS) was exactly that, not a way of guaranteeing needs satisfaction for the citizens of states. To vest "permanent sovereignty over natural resources" with the state does not guarantee any improvement in the livelihood of its citizens.[30]

In the same vein, there is the danger that what accrues to a group ends up with the group leaders; unless the state sees to it that collective goods to groups are not monopolized (like a village well on the land of the village landowner).

The meta-rule here would be that human rights are there to regulate relations between states and individuals, not between states and states, presumably the task of international (actually interstate) law. Human rights are supposed to make countries more transparent where relations between state and citizens are concerned. How a state treats its own citizens is no longer an internal affair but an international concern.

But the point made here is that the deeper factor standing in the way of group rights is not the elite fear of peoples strengthening their position through collective rights (although this certainly plays a role), but deep culture. As pointed out in chapter 1 and the first section of this chapter: Western cosmology defines individual actors as the ultimate units of the social construction, the social atoms or building bricks so to speak. In this perspective groups might not only constrain the free unfolding of individuals through obligations of solidarity; they are also less "real." Individuals are born, mature and die; but in between they are real, with inalienable rights. How can groups with no clear birth and death dates be capable of serving as norm-objects?[31]

We shall return to that in connection with the "solidarity rights" to development, clean environment and peace in chapter 4. Obviously, the right to development can be seen as the right to individual development, but also as a group right to the social development that makes individual development possible, including by removing obstacles.[32] The same will be shown to hold for clean environment, and for peace. The point made here is only that this cultural blindness to groups as holders of rights is *not* the same as the general structural blindness of the legal tradition. That tradition is based on issue-articulation, and behind the articulation are actors, in human rights cases victims who complain that their rights have been violated. Being actors they are likely to articulate themselves within an actor-orientated perspective. Complaints may lead to trials identifying evil acts and actors, and the rest of the story is in principle known. But what about complaints never aired because the harm and hurt are too deep inside the psycho-structures of the victims, and the social and world structures producing the wrongs are protected by "all do it; and have always done it?" Can we identify victims and violations when people are too used to being victimized to launch complaints, and no violators can be identified?

If building on tradition is insufficient let us go beyond tradition to the justification of norms, and human rights in particular, for an answer. There seem to be three approaches to justification: institutional, functional, and axiological.

The institutional approach would justify norms by referring to a norm-sender in no need of justification. In the Occident, with three revelation religions and the almighty revealing the laws to the prophet, the justification would be in terms of the almighty as norm-sender, granted that there can be interpretation problems. With increasing secularization, particularly in the Judeo-Christian regions of the Occident, justification would focus on the almighty's successors, as argued in chapter 1: the emperor/king, then the state with its various organs, and at the international level the community of states. For universal human rights, bridging that gap, justification would refer to the UN General Assembly and the human rights machinery.[33] The higher the community, the higher the rights.

The functional approach would justify norms by referring to the integrative impact of following the norms, and the disintegrative impact of breaking them for the social order in general.[34] Whereas the institutional approach identifies one institution as clearly above the rest, the others taking commands from that one, the functional approach is more horizontal. Norms are embedded in a fabric of institutions together constituting the social order or formation. Some norms can be broken by some without much consequence for the total fabric, but if broken by many, or many norms by some (not to mention many norms by many),[35] the social order may collapse. Disintegration may be easier to define than integration and may serve better for justification of norms. Norms can then be ranked according to the seriousness of the collapse following lack of compliance. In sociology and anthropology this is known as the functional approach.[36]

The axiological approach would justify norms by deriving them from higher norms or values.[37] This approach is already embedded in the other two, attributing supreme value to the almighty with successors, and to the "social order." Putting it this way, the problem with the first two approaches is evident: there has to be an element of faith, religious or ideological, in the authorities on top of the institution selected for justification as infallible; and that faith would then extend to the "social order" in the second approach. But religious people would not easily attribute infallibility to the secular order, or vice versa. Moreover, there are many religions and ideologies. And is social collapse always bad?

Added to that come the problems of the revealed norms, and the many readings of the revealed words. If the Ten Commandments were to be the basis, human rights would cluster around family values and property rights. The *sharia* in Islam is broader which may worry the other regions of the Occident: the *sharia* can stand up as a competitor. But in modern society a broader basis is needed than norms adequate for earlier social formations, and there is no separation between norm-creator, promoter, and monitor.

The problem is how to identify that broader value basis for human rights. One point of departure would be the word "human," asking why human beings should have rights at all? The other approaches might answer that question referring to humans as "God's children" or (very similar) as "citizens," *citoyens*; or as parts of the social order. Human beings exist less for their own sake than for the glory of the almighty, the state or the social order. Without human beings the state and the social order would be vacuous. And how about the almighty's creation if the pinnacle of that creation, in which the almighty injected so much drama through the knowledge of good and bad, the human beings, did not exist?

One value basis that would justify human rights in terms of human beings *per se* would be human needs. The approach can be broadened, building on the Buddhist tradition, to all life capable of experiencing suffering and bliss (*dukkha* and *sukha*).[38] The approach is problematic from the very beginning: how do we identify human needs? One answer: by asking people questions such as "What is it you cannot do without?" This is the approach that will be attempted in chapter 3.

One basic proposition in needs theory is, of course, that non-satisfaction has bad consequences. These consequences show up primarily in the human beings themselves, and may have ramifications on the surroundings. However, instead of referring to those surroundings as institutions or social orders the term used here will be "structure," in which human beings are embedded as actors, with more or less action space. Two typical reactions of human beings when suffering from needs deprivation would be passivity, even apathy, and then activity, even revolt. The former may ultimately lead to morbidity and mortality, perhaps also to alcoholism, drug abuse, mental disorder, and suicide. The latter may lead to outer-directed deviant social activity, such as criminal acts, perhaps homicide and political activity, including violent or non-violent revolution. Rulers tend to prefer the passive expressions of needs deprivation.[39]

These reactions may be interpreted, but certainly not unambiguously, as two very different ways of hitting at the structure: by emptying it through passivity and by challenging it through activity.[40] In other words, not only the analyst but also human beings in general may see the structure as one of the sources of their dissatisfaction and try to withdraw or to change it. But that gives us not only good reason to focus on social structures in general but also some idea of how to focus: by asking to what extent the structure produces needs satisfaction or needs deprivation, including when nobody intends it that way. And that will be the focus of chapter 4, on human rights and social structures.

Yet something is missing. The legal tradition can be accused of being (partly) structure-blind and culture-blind. But the legal tradition (or, better, traditions) is a fact of life, a part of the human condition. Needs and structures do not figure in that tradition, or at least not under those headings. That raises the problem of some kind of synthesis, which can come about only through a process. That process is already under way. Some aspects of that process, for instance who are the actors who can promote or delay that process, and how does that relate to the human rights we already have, will be the focus of chapter 5, on human rights and social processes.

Let us now come back to the question of identifying victims who do not articulate and violators who do not violate, or at least have no intention of doing so. *Human needs*, whether reflected in human rights or not, may serve as a guide to identify victims: where they are insulted human rights may have been violated or there may be a case for new human rights. At the same time, needs rather than rights direct us to look for causal factors rather than evil actors. As will be argued, certain social and world structures may be very important candidates, as sufficient if not as necessary conditions. Such structures, like slavery or colonialism (the US Declaration of Independence again!) will have to be changed. The problem is how this can be done within a legal tradition that probably will have even more difficulties handling structures (as opposed to actors) than groups (as opposed to individuals).

And this is where *process* enters. The human rights institution has been highly dynamic. Where are the next steps?

3

HUMAN RIGHTS AND HUMAN NEEDS

ON THE GENERAL RELATIONSHIP BETWEEN RIGHTS AND NEEDS

Given the rapidly growing interest in the theory and practice of human needs, the question arises: what is the relationship between human needs and human rights? Should human rights be seen as a special type of human needs, particularly related to the vast and problematic field of "freedom,"[1] or should they be seen as being two different kinds of things relating to each other in complex and important ways? The latter is the position taken here, and the argument is as follows.

Whereas human needs are seen as located inside individual human beings (and needs in general as inside live beings of any kind), human rights are seen as located *between* them. A human need is rooted in individuals and, we would add, in single individuals.[2] It is the individual who feels a need such as hunger, the satisfier of which is food. The individual, consequently, is the need-*subject*; the satisfier the need-*object*. If we accept that individuals are the only subjects that are capable of having a consciousness, then human needs are individual needs, although they certainly may, and usually do, require social arrangements for their satisfaction. Groups or any collectivity do not have needs: their members do. But they may struggle together for certain rights because the members have the same needs.

In fact, the satisfaction of needs has similarities with political processes in general: there must be some *consciousness*[3] of the need in the individual; this consciousness must become social and lead to some form of organization through mobilization; there is often some kind of confrontation to have the needs recognized; a real struggle to have the need satisfied may follow; and, finally, some form of transcendence whereby the need is satisfied individually and its sustained satisfaction more or less guaranteed/institutionalized socially.

Human needs may be classified in many ways,[4] but in the following the division of needs into the four groups of table 3.1 will be used. This is one approach. Other classifications of needs might lead to different – but probably not very different – conclusions.

Table 3.1 A typology of classes of needs, with antonyms

	Actor-dependent	*Structure-dependent*
Material	Survival (violence)	Well-being (misery)
Non-material	Freedom (repression)	Identity (alienation)

The distinction "material/non-material" can be interpreted two ways: as relating to the old body/mind distinction or somatic vs. mental (material vs. spiritual) needs; *or* as a question of whether the satisfaction of the needs requires material components or not. Thus, to satisfy such basic material well-being needs as food, clothing, shelter, medical treatment, and schooling, something material is obviously needed, meaning that there is a material economy of need-satisfaction. For a freedom need like the need to move, to have choice, or to express oneself; or an identity need like the need for a sense of meaning with life, it is doubtful whether in general anything material is needed at all. There can be identity with a national monument, but the image can suffice, whereas the image of food is hardly sufficient for needs-satisfaction. Admittedly the borderline is not a sharp one, nor does it have to be. We arrive at more or less the same result whether the need-subject or the need-object is taken as a point of departure for this distinction.

The distinction between actor-dependent and structure-dependent needs is equally important in understanding how to overcome needs deficits. In the first case something has to be done about actors whose deliberate acts impede the need-satisfaction of others; in the second case something has to be done about structures made in such a way that needs are not satisfied.[5] (Again, the borderline is not sharp.) The human rights tradition is, as will be argued, better suited to the first category, and consequently for survival and freedom needs, for reasons partly explored in the preceding chapter.

Human rights are, as mentioned, conceived of as *norms*; meaning located *between* actors, between a norm-sender (S) and a norm-receiver (R). S expects R to do or not to do certain things. In other words: S has an image of actions open to R in certain situations (R's action-space) and subdivides this space into regions of actions that, all the time according to S, are *prescribed*, *indifferent*, or *proscribed*, for R. R may not agree with this subdivision, and may not even agree that S has any right to structure the action-space for R at all. But we leave such problems aside for the moment in order to explore in more detail the (S, R, O) norm-triad model introduced in chapter 1;[6] including the actors whom the norm is actually about, the norm-*objects* (O). In other words, the need-*subjects*.

Thus, a human right has the following structure: S expects R to do/not to do something relative to O in general, and relative to the level of need-satisfaction of O in particular. This means that O has a claim on R, on something R should do (acts of commission) and/or something R should not do (acts of omission). Thus, O may expect R to provide employment and to abstain from torture. Further, since the expectations come from S, S may keep an account of how R is measuring up to those expectations; meaning that R may be accountable to S. Altogether this (S, R, O)-triad may be seen as the three corners in a social field constituting the expectations referred to as human rights, showing up as a *right* that may be claimed by O; as a *duty*, an obligation to live up to for R; and as an *expectation* from S. It should only be added, however, that any such triad exists in a social context, C. There are spectators and listeners, watching and observing what is going on – the triad is never or only under very extreme circumstances operating in a social vacuum. O can appeal to C when R, and even S, fails, for instance; C then being referred to as "public opinion," "world conscience," etc.

The question now becomes who are hiding behind these capital letters, and the possibilities are numerous. Some of these possibilities, 12 to be precise, are indicated in figure 3.1. They are listed from *individuals* at the bottom to *god* at the top. In between are various levels of social organization from what sociologists refer to as primary groups (kinship and friendship) and secondary groups (work organizations, schools, communities) to more complex levels of social organizations in structures characterized by assemblies (with varying geographical domains, from national via regional to the whole world) and/or executive authorities (with the same domains). Close to god is *logos*; reason, what is given as naturally obvious. The "Supreme Being" of the French 1789 Declaration may be a combination of the two.

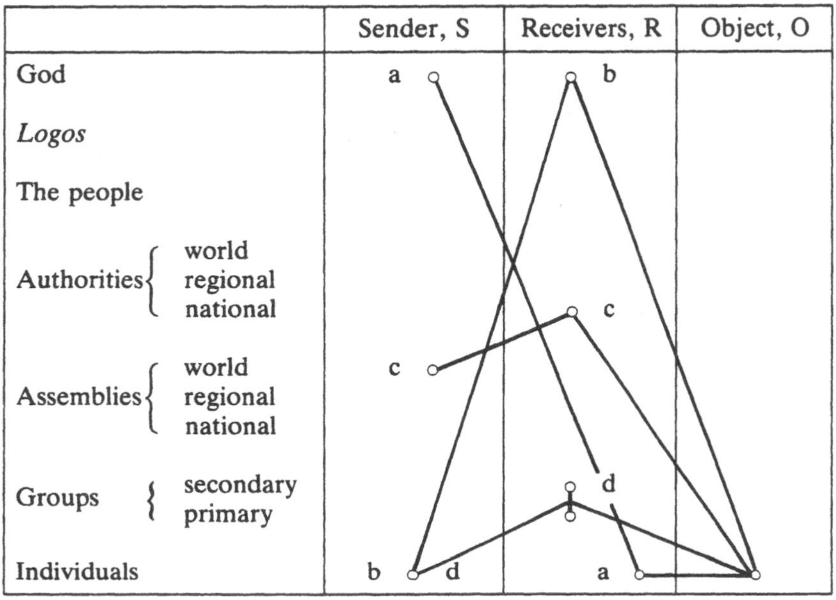

	Sender, S	Receivers, R	Object, O
God	a	b	
Logos			
The people			
Authorities { world / regional / national			
		c	
Assemblies { world / regional / national	c		
Groups { secondary / primary		d	
Individuals	b d	a	

Figure 3.1   The sender–receiver–object triad

In figure 3.1 four different types of rights triads are indicated, as examples. They all have one thing in common: the norm objects are individuals since these are seen as the only need-subjects.

In (a) god is the sender, individual human beings are the receivers and there are norms such as those expressed in the parable of the merciful Samaritan about the satisfaction of certain needs of other individuals. If R and O live in the same norm community and are both conscious of this, O may be said to have a certain claim on R, and R, in turn, is accountable to S.

In (b), exemplified by prayer, individuals express expectations to god, e.g. to alleviate the distress and misery of certain designated individuals, including S. In this model, according to Christian conceptions of God for instance, neither claims nor accountability are well established as the ways of God are held to be inscrutable.

These two examples serve as a sacred background for the secular combinations (c) and (d), the former being modeled after the Universal Declaration of Human Rights, the latter closer to much more commonly found norms all over the world. In (c) there is a world assembly, e.g. the General Assembly of the United Nations which on 10 December 1948 adopted the Universal Declaration that proclaimed particular sets of norms which, essentially, have as their receivers national authorities (governments). The norm-objects are individuals – usually referred to as "everyone" in the texts. In (d) the senders are seen as individuals and the receivers are all the groups, primary and secondary, of which the individual is a member or is in touch. The expectation is that these groups will take care of him or her, or of others for that matter.

Going back to the case of (c): the sender does not *have* to be the world assembly; as argued in chapter 1, it could also be a regional (for regional rights) or indeed a national assembly that makes laws binding on national authorities and citizens; after all, that is what legislation is about. Similarly, case (d) leads to other sender possibilities: the groups themselves, articulated in some kind of informal or formal meeting, or national assemblies/authorities that might expect, formally or informally, secondary and primary groups to take care of certain types of need-satisfaction. Much of this would be by tradition; that does not detract from the normative character.[7]

Many other combinations are possible. There is no need to spell them out to arrive at some more general conclusions. And those conclusions can be arrived at by asking one not very profound but very important question: whom would we prefer to see as senders, receivers and objects, respectively? As to the objects the answer has already been given: individuals – that is an almost consistent bias of the present analysis as pointed out in chapter 1.[8] But what about senders and receivers, beyond what was said in chapter 1?

There is in this phase of human history, inspired by Western concepts of universalism, a tendency to favor senders that are world assemblies (and not only the UN); or at least to use such senders, as Western countries have done, for codification and norm export. That tendency will be maintained to start with, with one important additional remark: the world assemblies could be representative of the expectations of peoples, not only of governments. We should think in terms of at least two more or less parallel channels through which expectations are sent, one at this world assembly, universal level, and another more rooted in common people all over the world. The ultimate conscience is the individual conscience, all the rest is abstraction. The question of attuning assemblies of any kind to the contradictory and controversial expectations held by billions of individuals will always be with us. As a problem it is unsolvable in an absolute sense, but not in the relative sense that there cannot be better or worse articulations at the world level of individual consciousness and conscience.

For the receivers there are also two models implicit in figure 3.1 if we disregard the theocratic models; one anchored in national (or regional, or world) authority, the other in civil society levels of social organization. Broadly speaking, they may be said to correspond to what elsewhere have been referred to as alpha-structures and beta-structures respectively,[9] the former being the large, usually highly vertical and fragmented structures typical of bureaucracies and corporations, the latter being small structures, not necessarily quite horizontal, but in a sense more à l'hauteur de l'homme.

What this amounts to is actually a distinction between a "higher channel" and a "lower channel" of human rights; one relating assemblies to authorities, and another relating groups/individuals to groups. These are the two major channels for satisfying human needs through human rights although only the former is referred to as such. We might refer to them as the alpha channel and beta channel respectively; and use them to anchor our thinking on needs and rights. Alpha is centralized and vertical, beta decentralized and horizontal. Alpha is male/abstract, beta is female/relational.

So far only one aspect of rights as norms has been explored: the (S, R, O)-triad. From this point we can now, following general norm theory, proceed in many directions in an effort to answer the question: what are the minimum conditions a norm has to satisfy to constitute a right? And could there be something in these conditions that would stand in the way of needs-satisfaction?

One very tentative list of such conditions, following the general logic of legal paradigms,[10] might look as follows:

1   *A process of norm production.*   In this process it is not enough to proclaim principles like "the right to food," or "the right to be

loved." These are exhortations, not directives structuring concrete action-spaces. A certain element of explicitness and of specificity are among the necessary conditions for norms to become rights whereby O has a claim on R, who in turn is accountable to S. Thus, a directive not to use fertile soil for purposes other than growing foodstuffs for local consumption (e.g. not for cash crops, not for housing and urbanization in general, not for roads and airports) would be an example of a norm inside a package of norms, more or less deductively organized, on which could be written "the right to food." As an example of a beta-channel norm could be given the adage, "if you have thoughts of love, do not be stingy with words of love," a possible norm inside a package of informal norms on which could be written "the right to be loved."

2 *Confirmation of norms.* There has to be some kind of stamp of approval or acceptance of the norms. The norm-senders must express that the work done conforms with their intentions; the norm-receivers that the norms have been received and understood as valid norms if not necessarily entirely agreed to; and, above all, the norm-objects must express their acceptance of the norms as instrumental to the satisfaction of their needs, if implemented. This type of consensus across the triad can often be obtained as long as one sticks to the level of exhortations (who is against the rights to food or to be loved?). The moment specific action directives held to be instrumental to the implementation of such principles are made explicit, consensus tends to decrease. The reason for this is not simply that only reasonably specific norms can have an impact on the choice of concrete actions, but also that the relationship between general principles and specific norms is a problematic one, as the examples above may serve to indicate. Such specifications are hardly ever necessary and sufficient conditions for the principles to be implemented. Usually they are neither necessary nor sufficient, but may have a relationship of high probability with the principles, given favorable conditions. And since conditions are often not favorable the probability may even be low.

3 *Application of norms.* The norms have to be applied, as they constitute a set of yardsticks defining the good society. Human rights can be seen as an ideology defining the good society. If such norms are lying dormant as a blueprint for a Utopia only, they will suffer from atrophy from not being applied (Durkheim's

Law). It is in their application and continuous testing that they become a part of the social process. Applied to concrete acts they can lead to one of three conclusions: that the action was in conformity with the norm, was indifferent relative to the norm, and that it was an infraction, not in conformity with the norm. It should be noted that for a norm to be applied it is not necessary that stage 2 above has been attained. A draft law or draft treaty does not have to be ratified by the appropriate body to be applied. The social context may come in as substitute sender if the local receiver (e.g. the local national assembly) has not yet ratified, or refuses to ratify, the norm, i.e. has refused to receive it, like the US refusal to ratify six major human rights instruments. These instruments are nonetheless a part of the context.

4 *Reaction to application.* A typical aspect of the legal paradigm is that there is reaction only in case of *infraction* of a legal norm. The public machinery, and discourse, is much richer in punishment than in rewards. As there is much evidence indicating that positive sanctions may sometimes be much more effective than negative sanctions, this should not be permitted to become an unquestioned aspect of the human rights approach. What matters is a system of sanctions, and sanctions can usually be divided into negative and positive, and personal and social. The personal sanctions, located inside the actor (R) will take the form of what in Christian parlance is referred to as bad vs. good conscience, as aspects or manifestations of an internalization process. The social sanctions are usually referred to as punishment and rewards, as manifestations of an institutionalization process. The more all four of these forms of sanctions are operating, the more could one say that the norm has become deeply rooted. Blaming the country with serious human rights deficits should not stand in the way of praising the country with a good record; with more mixed judgements for countries with mixed records, the majority. And words of blame and praise could be accompanied by other, more material, negative and positive sanctions. Prizes, citations.

5 *A machinery for adjudication.* It is customary to use this term to refer to infractions of the norms only, and according to this practice the adjudication would probably contain such elements as verification of the alleged infraction, conviction (which usually is in dichotomous guilty/not guilty terms), and a sentence if the actor is found guilty. Needless to say, the same formula could be used, substituting the terms worthy/not worthy for guilty/not

guilty if a more positive approach is taken. In either case there has to be a detection/reporting machinery.

6   *Administration of sanctions.*   If R is accountable to S, S will also have something to do with the administration of sanctions, not necessarily executing them, but in the sense of authorizing them. If these sanctions are negative, i.e. inflicting some kind of harm on R for having infracted human rights norms, the question is whether S has sufficient power to punish, meaning inflict some harm. A world assembly has limited power over national authorities, especially when the latter are major powers, even superpowers (and in addition can veto the authorization). A national assembly together with a national authority will have considerable power over R if R is a primary or secondary group. After all, basic to the whole idea of a state is power over at least most internal power relations.

Again we come back to the same problem: In the choice of (S, R, O)-triad a social and world formation is privileged as dominant. If S is higher in rank than R, S can probably control R more through negative sanctions than vice versa, but the result is the strengthening of the general control machinery at higher levels of social organization. If R is higher than S there is less opportunity to build excessive control machineries, but R is likely to convert its important role in implementing norms relating to needs to a virtual monopoly on important sectors of social activity related to needs-satisfaction (social work agencies may serve as examples). It may also be argued that R and S should be at the same level in order to have a dialogue on equal terms where one cannot outpower the other through authorization power or executive power. This argument would favor horizontal or nearly horizontal lines in figure 3.1, with higher level lines representing alpha channels, and lower level ones beta channels.

7   *Consonance approach.*   The goal of the administration of sanctions, in the legal paradigm, would be to have the actors act in conformity with the norms. There are the well-known, if not very realistic, theories of individual and general prevention; directed towards the actor who has already infracted a norm, and others who might do so because they are in or might come into the same position. To this should then be added a more realistic view: that some infractions are not seen as inadequacies in the actor, but as inadequacies in the norms, as pointed out in chapter 2 (see "Is the legal tradition culture-blind"). In this the epistemology of

empirical science is clearly visible: the map rather than the terrain could also be changed in case of discrepancy[11] between the two. Very important in this process would be the voices of O, who, as mentioned, should be strongly represented in both R and S from the very beginning since they are the needs subjects. Their weak presence in a representative system could make human rights an abstraction produced by people who never suffered needs deficits rather than a real source of needs-satisfaction.

8 *Validation of the entire process*.   As this is an ongoing, ever continuing process there must be some kind of authority that can validate the process – continuously, not only once and for all. Supreme courts and the International Court play such roles; so does the judgement of "history."

This list of eight criteria of "rootedness" is highly centered on the (S, R)-relation. The first two criteria deal with the sending of norms, and the next six in one way or the other with the problem of making R accountable to S. Again, what has happened to O for whose benefit the whole machinery is presumably made? Let us only repeat that O has to be present everywhere in this process, cooperating with S in the sending of the norms, and with R in their implementation. Since O is the one who knows best when and where the needs shoe pinches, O should also be in the position to detect deficits and to report to S about R. The moment R controls the detection machinery (i.e. the police), muting O through policies of repression, the human rights situation, is, as we know, precarious. Obvious conclusion: a free civil society is indispensable.

However, as hinted at above, there is also another way in which the human rights situation may become precarious: by excessive use of the alpha channel in defining (S, R, O)-triads. The alpha channel as a human rights approach to the implementation of human needs is institutional rather than structural, simply based on the usual interaction structure. It is based on the "freedom from fear" approach of protecting citizens against types of violence to human beings arising from the exercise of power within and between countries (states);[12] later on adding "freedom from want" (called "misery" in table 3.1). Then there is the "freedom to" approach of guaranteeing choices, e.g. in the important fields of expression and impression; of movement to and from, and association with, other people, and so on. The human rights approach is a social contract approach, the contract being between the citizens and the state. And this is where the doubleness of the state enters the picture, clearly seen with a little use of table 3.1. The state can protect, even guarantee needs-satisfaction; and can impede, obstruct, even destroy any chance of needs-satisfaction. The power of the state derives precisely from its Janus-faced character.

Thus, as is well known, the state can build institutions for security, referred to as the military and the police, to guard against external and internal sources of violence against the citizens. But these two institutions may, in turn, themselves become major sources of *in*security, when used for aggressive purposes without, and repressive purposes within.

The state, in the form of the modern welfare state, may use power, even monopoly power, over the use of the economic surplus, to satisfy well-being needs of its population. But the state may also use this power for elite consumption and privileges, for investment for the possible benefit of future generations, or for export in order to import, for instance, means of aggression and repression for the military and the police. The now defunct Soviet system used its enormous power over the economic surplus for all these purposes at the same time.

The state can serve as a guarantor of freedom, partly positively by enlarging the range of choices effectively available to the citizens in many fields of life, and partly negatively by controlling those who control others, e.g. men who batter their wives or abuse their children, instead of expanding their range of options. But the state may also do exactly the opposite: limit the range of alternatives, e.g. in the fields of what to say and write, and what to hear and read, partly through centralized censorship, partly by supporting types of authority lower down that may limit the range of options, such as churches and schools, media, schools of journalism. The road towards repression, here not in the sense of violence against citizens through torture or wanton killings by the state of its own citizens, but in the sense of limited freedom, does not necessarily use such machineries as the police and the military. Options can also be dramatically curtailed in the most "democratic" country where the state arrives at its decisions through a long process of attentive listening to alternative suggestions, ultimately ending up with one single compromise among contending factions, favoring none of them, but perhaps also satisfying none of them.[13] The road to repression can also pass through singularism as opposed to pluralism, favoring one structural answer to each functional problem instead of a multiplicity of answers. There are authoritarian and democratic ways of limiting the range of options. Repression as here conceived of is not the monopoly of authoritarian regimes, but presupposes a high level of centralized power, an alpha structure, in either case.[14] At the apex of that alpha structure executive power may be checked by legislative and judicial power. Alpha remains alpha; vertical and centralized, i.e hierarchical, and works about the same way in democracies and non-democracies.

Finally, the state can offer identity to its citizens by making them parts of a *corpus mysticum*, the ethos of which may be referred to as nationalism. The state can provide macro-identity, but can also serve to erode micro-identity. The latter can be done by instituting a terror regime whereby the alpha structure penetrates all small beta units with its detection machinery, with informers planted in all families, neighborhoods, at school, at work, in each community, and by organizing work so that most people become clients carrying out routine jobs, having their needs satisfied much like animals in a zoological garden.[15] Others define the action-spaces, both content and extension, rather than people working out action-spaces themselves, struggling with the natural and the man-made environment.

Alpha-dominated society becomes huge and distant and opaque. Closeness and transparency, as conditions for identity, recede into the background. The organization of work is structured in such a way that major decisions are taken centrally, in bureaucracies and/or corporations. Only routine implementations are left to people in general, in a standardized manner, thereby alienating people from their work products. The relationship of human beings to themselves and to others will probably also be more marked by alienation, thereby eroding other sources of identity. Much of this would stem from the use of the state to provide welfare, satisfying basic material needs, without taking into consideration that it is not only *that* these needs are satisfied but also *how* they are satisfied that matters.[16]

In short: the problem is not solved by making the state the recipient of an ever higher number of norms the implementation of which would lead to an ever higher level of satisfaction of some basic needs, adding to this adequate institutionalization through the various mechanisms discussed above. There is a cruel dialectic at work here: the more this machinery grows the more it may defeat its own purpose, not only through abuses when the machinery falls into the wrong hands, but through the very use, in a correct manner, of the machinery itself. More precisely: one may, as in the modern welfare state, gain in survival, welfare, well-being and freedom while at the same time losing in identity, buying the first three at the expense of alienation. The formal, institutionalized human rights approach is one approach to the satisfaction of human needs, by constituting institutionalized guarantees. But these institutions may also be a source of institutionalized non-satisfaction of the more non-material needs.

And that points again to the alternative human rights approach making use of the beta channel mentioned above, an approach often referred to as "informal," or as structural in the sense of being more built-in, more automatic, as reciprocal rights and obligations. An important dimension is indicated by the word-pair distance vs. closeness. The institutional approach is distant. The structural approach would be more based on closeness, on making the small (beta-)units surrounding the individuals major sources of need-satisfaction, reducing the relative significance of the higher levels of social organization, such as the national, regional, and world levels. For convenience these lower levels may be referred to as "local," and the attention then turns in the direction of patterns of local self-reliance.[17]

This is not the place to spell it out, only to argue the obvious, that smaller units *may* be much better at providing identity, or at least major forms of identity; and, if they have adequate control over the factors of production, also of providing for the satisfaction of basic material needs. The weakness is usually that such units are vulnerable to evil actors who may expose them to violence and repression, and also use this very fact as a basis for exploitation through the characteristic "bargain" of feudal societies: "You need protection, I am willing and able to protect you, but I need some compensation, for instance one half of everything you grow!" There is the understanding that if the offer is rejected violence and repression will follow immediately; in short, it is "an offer one can't refuse."[18] In many senses, including this one, the modern state is the successor of this aspect of the feudal systems, as has been repeatedly argued above. There is little or no choice; take it, or drop dead (or at least drop out.)

However, one may also conceive of other ways in which the needs for survival and freedom can be assured, at the same time preserving patterns of local self-reliance as the major sources providing welfare and identity. The general formula in this connection would be *confederalism*, not federalism with a set of strong institutions for finance, foreign and security/military policies in the center, but as a structural arrangement weaving units of local self-reliance not too tightly together (like the Nordic countries). The satisfaction of human rights would be built into a structure which in turn is based on the aggregate of billions of actions carried out by millions of individuals, in addition to basing it on explicit and specific norms directing designated actors to do something for somebody.

Needless to say, this is not a question of an either–or, of a choice between the alpha channel and the beta channel, between the formal and informal, between the institutionalized or the structural approaches. It is a question of both–and. But the basic insight would be that institutionalization of human rights as a means, although no doubt often productive in satisfying human needs (and that is the purpose of the whole exercise), may later become counterproductive simply because the institutions with their division of labor, penetration, segmentation, fragmentation, and marginalization will stand in the way. They are not neutral.

As mentioned, the human rights approach, as traditionally conceived of, is at its best in connection with the human needs referred to as survival and freedom. The reason for this is clear from table 3.1: these are the (more actor-dependent) needs that are most clearly threatened by deliberate acts of "evil" actors, whereas the other (more structure-dependent) needs are more often impeded by "wrong" structures. The borderline is not clear-cut and sharp, nor does it have to be. The point is simply that if the satisfaction of needs depends on the inclinations and actions of a relatively limited number of specific actors, then norms directed towards these particular actors as recipients are highly meaningful (which is not the same as saying that they are always effective).

But when the structure produces hunger, as the international agro-business structure may be said to do,[19] it may be less clear who the recipients of the norms should be. They are so many, so dispersed; so unaware of their own role. And above all, the relationship between their actions and the non-satisfaction of the need for food is very often indirect and tenuous. Precisely for these reasons there will be no feelings of guilt, no elements of bad conscience (which one would assume that the torturer has or at least has had at some point in his or her life) that human rights can hitch on to. Norms, against the use of soil for cash crops for example, may be merely experienced as unjust and as "ideological/political." And yet this is no doubt an approach. The right to food may be partly hedged around by a package of such norms, and these norms would then derive their legitimacy from the way they relate to satisfaction of basic human needs, rather than, or in addition to, the usual source of legitimacy: the enhanced nature of the norm-sender (god, *logos*, the people, authorities and assemblies of various levels).

To conclude: it is fruitful, even essential, to study the needs/rights interface. In the current situation there are needs that may be said to have rights counterparts; there are needs without rights counterparts leading to the idea of extending the concept of human rights; there are rights that do not have needs counterparts leading to the idea of certain cultural and class biases underlying the production of human rights; and there are no doubt relevant items that have not surfaced and become formulated explicitly at all, neither as needs nor as rights. There are all four possibilities. Moreover, the relationship between known needs and known rights is not a one–one relation. One identifiable need may be satisfied (wholly or partly) through the implementation of several rights; one right may be instrumental to the implementation of several needs. The relationship is not a simple and very neat one. In general the rights are the means, and the satisfaction of needs is the end, but like all other means–end relationships the relationship is complicated. To this we now turn.

WHICH RIGHTS SHOULD BE COMPARED WITH WHICH NEEDS?

In this exercise, a preliminary and exploratory one, something relatively well defined (rights) will be compared with something rather poorly defined (needs) according to principles that may be even more poorly defined, with the hope that something nevertheless can emerge from the exercise.

To start with, which are the human *rights*? The very useful compilation made by the United Nations, *Human Rights, A Compilation of International Instruments of the United Nations*, is what we want since the focus is on the UN as a norm-sender. In that book 41 instruments are presented under 14 headings. However, by far the most important category is found under the first heading, "The International Bill of Human Rights," where three instruments are grouped together:

1   Universal Declaration of Human Rights (UD);
2   International Covenant on Economic, Social and Cultural Rights (ESC);
3   International Covenant on Civil and Political Rights (CPR) (there is also the Optional Protocol to the CPR).

Since so much of what is found in the other instruments can be seen as specifications of the rights contained in these three the International Bill is used as a definition, in extension, of "human rights," perhaps even in the sense of "basic human rights." The word "basic," then, carries two connotations: "basic" in the sense that when the right is violated, the (negative) consequences (to the victim, not necessarily to the wrong-doer) are basic in terms of deprivation/destruction of basic human needs; and "basic" in the sense of being axiomatic in a (quasi-) deductive system. In the field of rights the latter connotation is important as deductions are in fact carried out (in the form of subsumptions). This is a part of the legal craft. In the field of needs deduction would only serve the purpose of organizing lists of needs, a process not necessarily corresponding to anything in the real world.

Then, which are the human *needs*? We shall use the list in table 3.2, which is a specification of the classes of needs given in table 3.1, so the needs are grouped in the same four classes. The list is the result of much trial and error, confrontations with literature, and dialogues with other researchers and, above all, with other people than researchers, etc.[20] There is no illusion that the list does not contain Western biases, but there is an assumption that at the higher level of abstraction of (four) needs classes (table 3.1) we can talk in terms of a certain universality. In one way or the other, survival, well-being, identity, and freedom make some sense all over the world even if the concrete interpretations may differ.

Each human being needs a minimum of survival, well-being, identity, and freedom. The universality disappears as the need formulations are specified as needs elements. The list is only a working hypothesis. It is tested by being used, in terms of criteria of fruitfulness, serving to identify problems already known to be important, and to guide us further in understanding problems that may become important one day but have not yet crystallized sufficiently.

Table 3.2 A list of basic human needs

Needs	Satisfiers held to be relevant in some societies
Survival needs – *to avoid violence*	
• against individual violence (assault, torture)	Police
• against collective violence (wars, internal, external)	Military
Well-being needs – *to avoid misery*	
• for nutrition, water, air	Food, water, airspace
• for movement, excretion, sleep, sex	
• for protection against climate, environment	Clothes, shelter
• for protection against diseases	Preventive, curative medicine
• for protection against heavy, degrading and boring work	Labor-saving devices
• for self-expression, dialogue, education	Schooling
Identity needs – *to avoid alienation*	
• for self-expression, creativity, praxis, work	Jobs
• for self-actuation, for realizing potentials	Jobs and leisure
• for well-being, happiness, joy	Recreation, family
• for being active and subject, not being passive, client, object	Recreation, family
• for challenge and new experiences	Recreation
• for affection, love, sex; friends, spouse, offspring	Primary groups
• for roots, belongingness, networks, support, esteem	Secondary groups
• for understanding social forces	Political activity
• for social transparency	Media
• for partnership with nature	Natural parks
• for a sense of purpose, of meaning with life	Religion, ideology
• closeness to the transcendental, transpersonal	Silence
Freedom needs – *to avoid repression*	
• choice in receiving and expressing information and opinion	Communication
• choice of people and places to visit and be visited	Transportation
• choice in consciousness-formation	Meetings, media
• choice in mobilization	Organization, parties
• choice in confrontation	Elections
• choice of occupation	Vocational schools
• choice of job	Labor market
• choice of spouse	Marriage market
• choice of goods/services	(Super-)market
• choice of way of life	Structural pluralism

How should we proceed in carrying out the comparisons? From the preceding section comes the idea of trying to identify four cases:

Table 3.3   Rights and needs: the four possibilities

1   needs with rights counterpart;
2   needs without rights counterpart;
3   rights without needs counterpart;
4   neither needs nor rights.

What we are comparing is, of course, neither needs nor rights, but formulations of either. Hence we are essentially looking for identical, synonymous or, more broadly put, equivalent formulations. The equivalence is not entirely semantic, though. Take as an example (UD, article 3) "everyone has the right to life, liberty and security of person," and compare it with "survival needs; against individual violence and against collective violence" giving as examples "assault, torture; wars internal and external." Obviously the two formulations are touching something of the same, and not only because "survival" and "security" are closely related. But they are not quite the same: there is the word "liberty" in the rights formulation, and some specification in the needs formulation. We would then scrutinize the needs list for something corresponding to "liberty," and the rights list for something corresponding to the specifications, and in this process it is more easy to identify dissimilarities than similarities. The latter are more open to doubts. Consequently, we shall start from the dissimilarity items – (2) and (3) in the list above.

HUMAN NEEDS WITH NO CORRESPONDING RIGHTS

With all the limitations of the method, let us compare the list of needs and the list of rights to arrive at some tentative conclusions. It is difficult because both lists are open to interpretations and, as mentioned, the needs are formulated in a rather general manner, whereas rights are subdivided, often with much precision. As a consequence several rights formulations might be relevant for one need formulation. The mapping is many to one. But even when all these rights formulations are juxtaposed they do not quite add up to the need formulation, which is usually richer in connotations.

Let us then proceed class by class on the list of needs.

Survival

There is the "right to life, liberty and security of persons" (UD, article 3) and the condemnation of the "cruel, inhuman or degrading treatment or punishment" (UD, article 5), the first being broad but certainly corresponding to the need formulation, the second being a very important specification. However, what about a right in connection with traffic accidents? What would be the impact on governmental policies of a *human right* not to die as the victim of society-generated accidents, and in this case not only in traffic but also at work (to some extent covered by ILO conventions) and at home? What effect would it have when deciding whether or not to build or extend a road adjacent to a school playground, for instance?

As to collective survival as opposed to attack or war, there is the Convention on the prevention and punishment of the crime of genocide. Genocide is defined in Article II as activity

> with intent to destroy, in whole or in part, a national, ethnical, racial, or religious group [by] killing members of the group, causing serious bodily or mental harm to them, inflicting on the group conditions of life calculated to bring about its physical destruction in whole or in part, imposing measures intending to prevent births within the group and forcibly transferring children of the group to another group.

One difficulty is that the need for survival, like all needs, is individually experienced; because only individuals can experience needs. The need does not discriminate between various types of intentions on the part of the attackers. From a survival point of view it is irrelevant whether the aggressor intends to eliminate just me, or me as a part of a larger group. But if the vision is expanded to include the need for identity with that group it becomes relevant. Hence, the genocide convention is a good case of a rights package that corresponds to a complex combination of needs for security and identity. It should, however, not be identified with a convention outlawing wars, and has the built-in danger that it might legitimize wars that fall short of eliminating substantial portions of groups, or do so without that "intent." In short, the genocide convention offers insufficient protection against collective violence.

Well-being

Whereas food is covered, (clean) air and water are not adequately covered by the rights; possibly because they were not on the agenda for those who drafted it. The same might be said in connection with the need for sleep. It is not enough to see it as partly covered by the right to rest and leisure (UD, article 24). Sleep is a very special type of physiological rest and several conditions have to be satisfied for sleep to take place, some of them incompatible with noise pollution and working patterns in modern industrial societies, for instance shift work. Some of the same certainly applies to sex.

Interestingly, the need for excretion cannot be seen to be covered either: possibly because many believe it is sufficiently well met not to constitute a problem in any society. But the point about need formulations is not necessarily that all needs have their counterparts in rights. A list of needs is a checklist of potential rights; if situations should arise when need-satisfaction can no longer be assumed to be automatically guaranteed. The foreigner in a city without public toilets knows what this means; so do the very poor in a city center. Under what conditions would a sufficient number of people make this basic need get a human rights counterpart?[21] When the drafters are threatened by the same needs-deficits in the fields of sleep, sex, and excretion?

What about the need for some kind of protection against excessive strain, or in general against work (not only punishment) that can be said to be excessively dirty, heavy, cruel/inhuman/degrading, and boring? In this particular basic rights instrument such needs are not covered, and even if covered by ILO conventions the point could be made that the need is so important that it should be reflected in more basic instruments. But sharing working conditions more equitably would upset our entire society. And the same applies to needs for education in the sense indicated in the list of needs: as self-expression, as dialogue; not only as the need to be taught idiom and culture, and some other basic tools for survival in the society in which the individual has been born. Of course, there is much about education (ESC, article 13), such as the recognition of the right of everyone to education. The formulations are beautiful: "Education should be directed to the full development of the human personality in the sense of its dignity, and should strengthen the respect for human rights and fundamental freedoms." What is missing, however, is the dialogical aspect, education of Self together with Others, for other- and self-development. In a sense the instrument is too institutional; seeing people as raw material with the right to be adequately processed by the institution for education: the school.[22]

Freedom

Whereas freedom of expression is extremely well covered (UD, article 19) in the classical human rights, freedom of impression is not given equally explicit attention.[23] It may be argued that if there is freedom of expression there will also be freedom of impression. If people are free to express what is on their mind, that freedom would include the freedom of others to be impressed by what is expressed. The freedom of others to express whatever one wants inside a prison cell with nobody listening is not the freedom of expression intended in the Universal Declaration. However, the matter is not quite that simple. There might be freedom of expression and yet everybody might be expressing the same thing because they have been shaped the same way. This is where the freedom of impression would go one step further and demand a richer, more diverse environment of impressions. There is, possibly, a parallel to this under "freedom of movement" (UD, article 13). On the one hand it would imply one's own freedom to visit whatever and whomever one wants to visit. But it is not so obvious that it implies the freedom to be visited by whomever one wants. If everybody enjoys freedom of movement, the freedom to be visited by whomever should be implied: "movement" implies more than "expression" and "holding opinion." Listening and reading/viewing are as important as speaking and writing.

The political freedoms of consciousness-formation, mobilization, and confrontation are to a large extent covered by the freedoms of assembly and association (UD, article 20(1)–(2)) and trade union formation (UD, article 23(4)). The difficulty, however, would be that these rights steer the political process in the direction of Western institutionalization. The need in this connection is the need for empowerment, and more particularly for the power to change the system in such a way that it serves the satisfaction of other needs better.[24] For this to happen consciousness about how the society and the world function, concerted action and non-violent confrontation for change are, if not sufficient, at least necessary ingredients.

But these are general formulations that should then be compared with the logic of a democratic election: consciousness may be raised by the campaign, but it may also be distorted if the political parties competing for attention are too similar and the campaign is person- rather than issue-orientated. Or, the consciousness-formation market emphasizes the less important and de-emphasizes the more important issues. Parties are ways of mobilizing and organizing people, but they may also be ways of disciplining and demobilizing them. Elections are ways of expressing power, but they are also very individualizing and may impede a more organic process of consensus formation dividing society between a winning majority (or plurality) and a losing minority. Humankind has probably not come very far in understanding the political process, or how particular ways of institutionalizing that process may also be counterproductive. Thus, article 25(b) of the CPR may be too specific.[25]

Such other freedoms as the choice of spouse, place to live, and occupation are well covered (see UD, articles 13, 16(2) and 23(1)), but not well. Rather important would be the freedom to experiment with alternative social formations, and the freedom to have a richer choice in ways of life. In very general terms the way of life is the way of distributing basic activities (such as work, leisure, eating, sleeping, etc.) in space, in time, and in social space, a question of *what is done where, when and with whom.*[26] All known societies can be said to limit this freedom, to regiment and discipline the distribution of activities at least to some extent. But this is a rather serious limitation when everybody has more or less the same working hours, the same meal hours, the same number of years of childhood education, work, retirement, etc.

What would be the range of options that would provide real choices for the citizens of a society? And what would be the impact on societies if the right to experiment with alternative ways of life were better institutionalized? One might venture the guess that the implications would be rather important, that a society rich in experience derived from experiments is much better positioned to straddle crises than a society which harbors no such experiments, only replicating itself from one day to the other, homogeneous from one point in space to the other, and for that reason with no alternative to draw upon in case it is badly hit by natural and social catastrophes.

Identity

Identity is perhaps the general needs area where there is most discrepancy between needs formulations and rights formulations. Expressed differently: whereas the needs language is relatively rich, the rights language seems to be poor. And this is not only a question of semantics. There is no doubt that large areas of needs are uncovered by rights, whatever the consequence or the cause might be.

Thus, to start with the identity with the work product: there is the famous formulation (UD, article 27(2)) to the effect that "everyone has the right to the protection of the moral and material interests from any scientific, literary or artistic production of which he is the author." This may be interpreted as the right to have some control over the surplus value produced by some particular type of non-material production. The right points in the direction of patents and copyrights, and the many activities engaged in by artists, particularly in the field of music. As such it is the expression of the interests of a particular class of workers: cultural workers. This class is well represented among the people who exercise significant pressures on the norm production in connection with human rights. It is actually the only professional group mentioned in the Universal Declaration.

But how about workers in general? We have stipulated a general need to have identity with one's own work product, and that would certainly not only go beyond the category of remuneration, well into the "moral interests," but also beyond the category of cultural workers to producers in general. The strong position of the human rights tradition in favor of the family may imply that the type of "production" that goes on inside the family, including in the form of reproduction, is protected in the sense that parents retain a relation to their "work product," their offspring.[27]

If reproduction were organized in society the same way as production in general, the offspring would be taken away immediately after birth to be marketed. The moral indignation when such practices are known to occur, e.g. under conditions of slavery or extreme misery where the parents sell their children as slave labor (or even for transplants) or for prostitution, or for adoption (this, at the international level, being the modern form) is an expression of the feeling that there *is* an organic tie between parents and offspring, workers and product. But what about this tie in the more general case? Why is there no expression in the Universal Declaration of Human Rights that reflects the umbilical cord between workers and work products in general? Not even for individual artisans, when it is done for individual artists? Why do artists and authors have the right to put their names on paintings and books, but workers not on cars?

The explanation is, of course, that such upgrading of workers might smack of socialist egalitarianism, and the Universal Declaration is not a socialist document. But it is interesting to speculate on an extension or reformulation of article 27(2) in the direction of, for instance, "everyone has the right to the protection of the moral and material interests resulting from any kind of work product to which he or she has contributed with their work."

To this it may be objected that there is a key phrase in article 27(2), "of which he is the author." Leaving aside the male chauvinism inherent in this expression, the basic point is the one–one relationship between the individual cultural worker ("author" is in the singular, the plural possibility of a team is not even alluded to) and the work product. The objection would be that in the case of factory work, for instance, there is no such one–one relationship. But factory work can be organized in a different way as shown by the Sony and Volvo (and many other) experiments whereby individual workers assemble the total product. They are not signing it, however; an interesting expression of limits to blue collar worker identity with work products.[28] If this is changed in the future an important border between the artistic, artisanal, and industrial modes of production would be blurred.

However, it may also be objected that this reasoning is a way of playing up to the individualism inherent in article 27. Why should not the collectivity of workers, especially in a team, have the "right to the protection of the moral and material interests" of a collectively produced work product, or set of work products? More concretely, this would mean both the right to decide over the material surplus produced through their work, and the right to be identified with the work product, to feel pride in it, to be criticized positively or negatively, on the basis of the work product. Today, bridges and major buildings are identified not with the workers, but with the architect who made the drawings, possibly with the name of the engineering firm, in many cases with the bureaucrats or politicians who made the decisions or cut some seal at inauguration ceremonies. Thus, there is space for improvement in this field. The way it has been done so far should not be seen as the final formulation, but as carrying the class signature of those who drafted the formulations.

However, there are more aspects to identity than identity with the work product. Identity with oneself is of key significance, particularly in individualist societies. One way in which this identity is threatened is through the overt and covert data collection on individuals taking place in modern societies yielding a multiple, but always segmented view of the individual personality. One agency or company has some data, another some other data, and even when all these data-sets are brought together (in accordance with or against the regulations stipulated in that society) the total data profile may give a presentation of the person, but not the self-presentation that person would have given of himself or herself. Leaving aside the problem of whether some of the data might be wrong or misleading, assuming that each data element is correct, the inner coherence between the data elements, the themes of which the data elements may be seen as expressions of the underlying personality, may differ profoundly from the themes that constitute the person's self-image.

Hence, the right of an individual to self-presentation, to *Selbstdarstellung*,[29] as it is called in German, should be an inalienable right. The individual might say "yes, it is correct that I did that and that I said this, but it was because . . ." This right seems to be better protected under the legal concept of "due process of law," at least in countries where this tradition can be said to be well institutionalized, than in connection with data banks to which the individual may not even have any access.[30] Or, if he or she has access it would at most be to try to correct misleading information, not to give his or her version, like a more holistic picture, with the underlying "theme," psychological or religious/ideological.

What about the right to identify as a community with others? Interpreted as cultural identity it is well covered by the human rights tradition. However, it should be pointed out that "others" is then interpreted in the direction of nations rather than other major groups, such as gender and generation groups, or classes and races. They are not legally defined (UD, article 15).[31] And some of them may for many be as important, or more important, than nations.

The right to identity with society can be said to be covered in many ways. But there is at least one way in which it is not covered: the right to understand social forces, the right to *social transparency*. It may be said that much of this is at least attempted to be covered under rights that guarantee freedom of expression, also about social and political matters. But this goes beyond abstract analysis of social forces. Some kind of transparency is needed, to interpret what is going on by sufficient insight into what in fact is happening, and above all what is being planned. This does not mean unlimited access by the public in general, and social scientists, and media in particular, to the inner working of all decision-making machineries, or unlimited access by everybody else to the writings by social scientists. This is not a call for total demystification of society; that is meaningless and some might even feel that this approach would only mystify society further. But there should not be too much of a gap between the image of society held by the elite and the view of the same society held by the people, by those not in power. The people should have a right to exercise some influence on how society is presented, and indeed on how it is planned. Democracy is meaningless without transparency. The condition: independent media.

In these three human rights instruments there is nothing about identity with nature except some references with a clear economic content. It should be pointed out, however, that identity with nature is not the same as access to nature, or the same as non-economic uses of nature, e.g. for recreation, aesthetic stimulation, etc. Identity with nature would go deeper; including a feeling of oneness with nature, of not being separated from nature by a gap between *Herr* and *Knecht*. It may imply the guaranteed right to withdraw from society into nature, living like a hermit; or living in very small communities surrounded by vast nature. The world might even be too small if this right were accorded to everybody. But it may also be interpreted as the right not to be forced into *Herrschaft* rather than *Partnerschaft* relations with nature, for instance by having to participate in industry-based economies, having to eat biochemically treated food and so on. Such rights, when implemented, might be very soft on nature and for that reason highly compatible with the limited world in which we live, particularly given the expanding population.[32]

Identity in the sense of having a purpose, or meaning with life, or closeness to something transcendental and transpersonal can be seen to be partly covered by the rights protecting organized religion (UD, article 1). But again there is the same problem: organized religion might also stand in the way rather than facilitate the satisfaction of these existential needs. Maybe we know too little about the conditions under which such needs are satisfied. One guess would be that in a highly alienating society a sense of purpose with life is being lost, in which case there should be a right to have access to non-alienated work; interpreted as creative work, meaning work with uncertainty built into it so that decisions have to be made. Something has to be shaped, created, beyond implementing routine rules.

A right to access to creative work would be an important human right that might serve to satisfy the need for a purpose of life, or indeed a need for identity with something above oneself. Might, perhaps. A negative perspective might be more realistic. The most the human rights tradition can do, and that is already a great deal, is to identify the negative conditions that when not satisfied would lead to the non-satisfaction of a need. Among them the right to exercise organized, institutionalized religion is one, and the right to have access to creative work may be another. The latter would no doubt be resisted by those in society who for all practical purposes have monopolized that right: creative, intellectual elites; some of them found inside the organizations known as bureaucracies and corporations,[33] most of them found in the universities, academies, and free professions of various kinds. But guaranteed access does not mean that people make use of it, or that gratification follows if they do.

In short: even given the very limited perspective on needs presented in the preceding section it is quite clear that there are important gaps between needs and rights, both in general terms, and in terms of major groups of the population. The agenda for future human rights is rich, and the needs approach is fruitful in legitimizing the entry of new items on to that agenda.[34] But the final sense of gratification is within each individual and is highly subjective. Consequently we are talking about necessary rather than sufficient conditions.

Human rights with no corresponding needs

Let us now review the three human rights instruments with a view to uncovering rights formulations that cannot be said to have any clear needs counterpart. As will be pointed out later, that is not necessarily any criticism of the concept of rights. There is no reason to have a complete correspondence between the two concepts. The position taken is that in so far as development is associated with progressive satisfaction of human needs, and human rights are seen as an instrument of development, then there will have to be *some* correspondence.

To start with the most famous formulation:

UD:1   *All human beings are born free and equal in dignity and rights. They are endowed with reason and conscience and should act towards one another in a spirit of brotherhood.*

Comment   This is obviously not a needs formulation. It can be seen as a mixture of a description and a normative statement about how human beings behave. As such, the statement leaves something to be desired: there is no recognition of what one might call the animal part of man. If the statement had started with a description of human beings as an inextricable web of body, mind and spirit, of the biological and the social, the physiological and the cultural,[35] then it would serve as a basis for references to human needs, provided one assumes that these are the interrelated sources of human needs. Out of these sources "reason and conscience" may arise, but to say that *all* human beings "should act towards one another in a spirit of brotherhood" is probably to go far beyond the limits to human compassion.[36] As such, this statement is compatible with a Christian tradition, very spiritual and very universalist, but also very unrealistic. And, as an important aside: where is sisterhood? And do siblings always constitute ideal models?

UD:2   *Everyone is entitled to all the rights and freedoms set forth in this declaration, without distinction of any kind, such as race, color, sex, language, religion, political or other opinion, national or social origin, property, birth or other status.*

Comment   This is not a formulation of needs either but an excellent statement of social justice; the idea that ascribed variables such as those listed should not have any influence on a person's access to social goods.[37] The article actually goes on to stipulate that the political status of the territory in which a human being lives shall not serve as a basis for making distinctions relative to human rights either. And articles 6, 7 and 8 carry the social justice formulation further, relative to access "to equal protection of the law." The same applies to articles 9 to 12, with the possible exception that article 9 ("No one shall be subjected to arbitrary arrest, detention or exile") also has to do with the freedom of movement. Obviously, the word "arbitrary" is the key word in the article: there may be arrests, but only if they are in accordance with due process of law.

What about the following articles, however?

UD:15   *1)   Everyone has the right to nationality.*
2)   No one shall be arbitrarily deprived of his nationality nor denied the right to change his nationality.

Comment   We have stipulated a need for group belongingness, and not only to primary groups directly surrounding the individual, but also to secondary groups such as nations. However, whereas the nations of the world can be counted and listed, the concept of a "secondary group" is much broader. To have a nationality may be neither a necessary nor a sufficient condition for this need to be satisfied. And again there is no corresponding formulation about the right to belong in an organized way to other large groupings, such as gender groups, generation groups, races and classes, territorial and non-territorial groups. It may be objected that this is because they are "tertiary groups," classifications rather than groups with internal interaction. But this is only true under conditions of very low levels of consciousness. The transition from category to secondary group is linked to such political phenomena as social mobilization, usually based on consciousness-formation as happened with gender during the 1970s and 1980s.

The formulation in UD:15 reflects a limited and perhaps also old-fashioned perspective of group belongingness, however important it is. Again the nation state is privileged, through the human rights tradition, seeing the nation as need-satisfier, and the state as guarantor. How about those for whom gender and class solidarity are much more important?

UD:16   *1)   Men and women of full age, without limitation due to race, nationality or religion, have the right to marry and to found a family. They are entitled to equal rights as to marriage, during marriage and at its dissolution.*
3)   The family is the natural and fundamental group unit of society and is entitled to protection by society and the State.

Comment   The last point in this article goes far beyond needs theory in emphasizing the family. The concept of "marriage and its dissolution" is probably also too specific to be said to correspond to needs. Thus, one might ask how homosexual unions (including marriage), social adoption, non-marital sexual relations, communal living, etc. would fit into these formulations, unless interpreted as sufficient conditions for the satisfaction of a bundle of needs traditionally associated with the family. The formulation limits the range of satisfiers.[38]

UD:17   *1)   Everyone has the right to own property alone as well as in association with others.*
2)   No one shall be arbitrarily deprived of his property.

Comment   It seems quite clear from the formulation that what is referred to here is *private* property, individual and "in association with others" (opening for collective property?). It would be difficult to postulate a general need to have private property in any kind of universal sense. Even in the most property-conscious countries the *need* to have property seems to be limited. Thus, very few seem to feel that it constitutes an infraction of their rights not to have their own private tram, for instance, running around on city tracks according to a schedule stipulated by the owner. Hence, the justification for this article will have to be found somewhere else,[39] for instance in the Roman law concept of *dominium*. Or, as for the emphasis on family in UD:16, in the Ten Commandments in the Judeo-Christian tradition.

UD:21   *1)   Everyone has the right to take part in the government of his country, directly or through freely chosen representatives.*
2)   Everyone has the right of equal access to public service in his country.
3)   The will of the people shall be the basis of the authority of government; this will shall be expressed in periodic and genuine elections which shall be by universal and equal suffrage and shall be held by secret vote or by equivalent free voting procedures.

Comment   Again the same discrepancy between the general need for participation in any political process concerning oneself, through consciousness-formation, mobilization, and confrontation, and (in paragraph (3)) a very special institutionalization of this based on the (Western) system of parties and elections, underlying which there is an ethos of political individualism. Where is democracy by consensus, obtained by dialogue until consensus is obtained?

    UD:21(1) and 21(2) are actually social justice norms, and as such hardly expressions of needs, but of values governing the construction of social structures. The rights discourse is at this point simply richer than the needs discourse.

UD:23   *1)   Everyone has the right to work, to free choice of emloyment, to just and favorable conditions of work and to protection against unemployment.*

UD:24   *Everyone has the right to rest and leisure, including reasonable limitation of working hours and periodical holidays with pay.*

Comment   Here is a clear distinction between work and leisure, well
known from Western industrialized societies, that cannot be
seen as an expression of a need either. Rather, there might be a
need for some integration between work and leisure, perhaps
not a basic need, but something not reflected in these rights
formulations. If leisure = pleasure, why should we not have
work = pleasure and leisure = work? Is there a hidden
assumption that work has to be cruel/inhuman/degrading – and
boring? It should be added that there is also article 23(2), which
is a norm of social justice, stipulating equal pay for equal work,
and an article 23(3) that ties remuneration for work to the ideal
of "ensuring for himself and his family an existence worthy of
human dignity." The male language used makes it clear who is
supposed to be the bread-winner, and the reference to the
family also ties remuneration for production to the idea of
reproduction. Again, it is difficult to see that these are expressions of needs, and certainly not of women's or children's
needs. They are expressions of patriarchical, family-based
social orders. But then there is no assumption that the political
ideology of human rights should be limited to basic human
needs alone.

UD:26   *3)   Parents have a prior right to choose the kind of education
that shall be given to their children.*

Comment   This may express a need of parents, at least in many cultures,
but not necessarily a need of children. The family is seen as a
society within the society, with the parents having legislative,
executive and judicial powers. As such it sounds quaint. But it
serves as a protection of an important small beta (or gamma!)
structure, the family, against big society alpha penetration.

UD:28   *Everyone is entitled to a social and international order in which
the rights and freedoms set forth in this Declaration can be fully
realized.*

Comment   This admirable formulation provides an excellent linkage
between various levels of social organization, from the individual levels at which these rights are seen to be implemented or
violated, toward the structure of the social and world spaces. It
stipulates conditions, or indicates the spaces in which these
conditions may be identified, rather than the needs. The needs
are inside the individual, but the conditions for their satisfaction are social or international, generally speaking.[40] The
implementation of this article relative to the International Bill
of Rights would be nothing short of revolutionary. Go ahead!

UD:29   *1)   Everyone has duties to the community in which alone the free and full development of his personality is possible.*

Comment   A relatively empty formulation as long as the duties are not specified. But what is being said is very significant: *there are no rights without duties*, as pointed out in chapter 1. But again this does not necessarily correspond to a need except as a possible need also to have duties, and be socially useful by living up to these duties. But human beings can hardly be said to be born into strict distinctions between rights and duties; that distinction is analytical rather than empirical. Incidentally, it is interesting to see that the word "community" (not "nation" or "country") is used as the setting "in which alone the free and full development of his personality is possible." This is probably very realistic: human beings developed their personalities long before anything corresponding to "countries" (run by states, peopled by nations) in our sense existed, whereas "communities," given a broad definition, are as old as humankind itself.[41] The formulation points to the beta channel, to the small rather than the big.

Let us then move on to the International Covenant on Economic, Social and Cultural Rights. The ESC actually does not bring in so many new ideas; but some of the reformulations are interesting. It is written in four parts, of which Part IV (articles 16 to 31) stipulates how reporting should be done, and how the United Nations enters into the picture.

ESC:1   *1)   All peoples have the right to self-determination. By virtue of that right they freely determine their political status and freely pursue their economic, social and cultural development.*
2)   All peoples may, for their own ends, freely dispose of their natural wealth and resources without prejudice to any obligations arising out of international economic co-operation, based upon the principle of mutual benefit, and international law. In no case may a people be deprived of its own means of subsistence.

Comment   One important point here is the formulation in terms of "all peoples"; in other words, in terms of collective rights rather than the individualism alluded to in the "everyone" of the Universal Declaration of Human Rights. Article 1(2) has the important final clause, "in no case may a people be deprived of its own means of subsistence," which points directly towards the New International Economic Order. And this becomes even more clear in the formulation in article 2(3): "developing countries, with due regard to human rights and their national economy, may determine to what extent they will guarantee the economic rights recognized in the present Covenant to non-nationals." Is this one reason the United States is withholding ratification? What about Native Americans and indigenous peoples everywhere?

ESC:7   *(c) Equal opportunity for everyone to be promoted in his employment to an appropriate higher level, subject to no consideration other than those of seniority and competence.*

Comment We cannot talk about a need to be promoted, in a general, universal sense. Leaving the social justice aspect aside, this may be a typical case of how a universal human right may serve to constitute a universal human need where there was no such thing in advance, by promoting a way of organizing employment that rules out both caste organization and horizontal organization as possible social structures. Individual ("everyone" again!) promotion becomes the universal rule. What about the right of a group that works very well together to be promoted as a group?

ESC:10   *1) The widest-possible protection and assistance should be accorded to the family, which is the natural and fundamental group unit of society, particularly for its establishment and while it is responsible for the care and education of dependent children. Marriage must be entered into with the free consent of the intending spouses.*

Comment An even more clear exhortation of the family as the pillar on which society is built than was found above in UD:16(3). But then the family is basic to the Ten Commandments in the Judeo-Christian faith, but not, for instance to the Noble Eightfold Path of Buddhism.

ESC:12   *1) The State Parties to the present Covenant recognize the right of everyone to the enjoyment of the highest attainable standard of physical and mental health.*
2) The steps to be taken by the State Parties to the present Covenant to achieve the full realization of this right shall include those necessary for:
(a) The provision for the reduction of the still-birth rate and of infant mortality and for the healthy development of the child.
(b) The improvement of all aspects of environmental and industrial hygiene.

    (c) *The prevention, treatment and control of epidemic, ende-*
    mic, occupational and other disease.
    (d) *The creation of conditions which would assure to all*
    medical services and medical attention in the event of
    sickness.

Comment It is interesting to see that by now everyone is entitled to "the enjoyment of the highest attainable standard of physical and mental health," which seems to be more than UD:23(3)'s "an existence worthy of human dignity," and UD:25(1)'s "a standard of living adequate for the health and the well-being of himself and of his family." However, the most important part of this article is the explicit role given to the state (as opposed to other levels of social organization), in other words to the alpha channel mentioned in the opening section of this chapter.

We then proceed to the International Covenant on Civil and Political Rights, to which many of the comments made above may also apply. It is also organized in four parts, of which Part IV does not stipulate human rights but serves to create a machinery. The covenant is written in "everyone" language rather than in "all peoples"-language, and in many cases the formulations are similar to the Universal Declaration.

CPR:20 *1) Any propaganda for war shall be prohibited by law.*
2) Any advocacy of national, racial or religious hatred that constitutes incitement to discrimination, hostility or violence shall be prohibited by law.

Comment These cannot be said to be expressions of needs either. On the contrary, if there is a need for identity related to belongingness to nations, races or religious groups, then hostile attitudes and verbal or non-verbal expressions *may* be ways of satisfying this need. They are negative ways and harmful to the needs of others for identity with *their* groups, and hence a clear case of conflicting needs where rights might steer and regulate.

CPR:24 *1) Every child shall have, without discrimination as to race, color, sex, language, religion, national or social origin, property or birth, the right to such measures of protection as are required by his status as a minor, on the part of his family, society and the state.*
2) Every child shall be registered immediately after birth and shall have a name.

3)   Every child has the right to acquire a nationality.

Comment   It is interesting to see that at this stage children are endowed with some rights, although only "measures of protection as are required by his status as a minor"; not more positive rights (such as survival, or the access to work without being exploited). From being subjugated to the will of the parents at least as regards education the child can here be seen on his or her way toward full personhood, probably meaning adulthood.

To explore this further, let us now change the perspective. So far we have compared lists of needs formulations with lists of rights formulations, with a view to locating overlaps and discrepancies, reflecting on why the two lists relate the way they do. In that type of approach there is a built-in danger: an assumption to the effect that there *should* be a very high degree of overlap. In other words, that rights should be based on needs; needs presumably being the more basic of the two. This is no doubt one fruitful perspective. But, as some of the reflections above have shown, "needs" and "rights" are perspectives of different kinds; they both constitute valid approaches to the human condition. Hence, the problem is to identify not only lack of overlap, but also ways in which these two approaches may be contradictory because one stands in the way of the other.

SOME WAYS IN WHICH NEEDS MAY COUNTERACT RIGHTS

The question this time is the opposite of the preceding section: not how will needs inspire rights, but how may needs distort rights?

First, there is one obvious answer: needs are defined at the individual level. The position taken here is that needs exist at the individual level only because a need-*subject* is required, and the only subjects known are individual beings, and for human needs (the concern here), individual human beings. But that limits the perspective on goals of development, or "progress." To take one example: the theme of equality. We may postulate a need in human beings for a basic *minimum* of satisfiers of various needs. But it seems hard to postulate a *need* for equality in the sense that human beings would break down, disintegrate one way or the other unless all human levels of need-satisfaction were about the same. Some might in fact postulate a need for inequality, but we are not doing that either. Rather, the position taken here would be that these are social system characteristics rather than individual characteristics, and that system characteristics relate to values embedded in ideologies embedded in cultures, and not necessarily to needs as experienced by individuals.

This, on the other hand, shows us the advantage of higher-level norm-receivers and the alpha channel. Only those that are at a higher level will be in a position to have a regulatory impact on such system characteristics as equality, social justice, and diversity built into the social structure. For all of these there may be some distant parallels at the individual need level. There is the need of women to have "education." But that is not the same as the "need" of all women to have an educational distribution that would coincide with the educational distribution for men. Similarly, there might be a need for "new experience." But that is not the same as a system level guarantee of diversity built into society, with ample opportunity for mobility. for those who want to move. There is no immediate translation from needs to social distribution and social structure. There are ambiguities, interpretations, functional equivalents and things of that kind that will make the relationship very different from any kind of strict deduction in the mathematical sense. For that reason the class of rights is broader than the class of needs in the sense of covering states of affairs that do not necessarily meet needs directly. It also *should* be broader, playing on various social conditions that in and by themselves may be *sufficient* to meet needs (which is then quite different from being *necessary* conditions).

Second, and very much related to this: needs are defined at the individual level; rights may be individual rights but could also be *collective* rights (group rights). These are not the same as rights concerning the organization of social or world systems, whether the latter is a sufficient condition for meeting needs or not. These would be rights that concern the collectivity *as an actor*, among other collectivities. The right of a minority to run their own school is, as mentioned, *not* the same as the right of minority individuals to have access to majority schools. The "rights of nations" and the "rights of states" would also belong in this category. A famous "right of nations" is the right of self-determination, and one of the most famous "rights of states" from recent times is associated with the New International Economic Order (NIEO), e.g. as expressed in the Charter of Economic Rights and Duties of States. An analysis of this charter[42] makes it clear that the norm-sender is the United Nations, and the norm-objects are the states. But who are the norm-receivers? They would be something between the states in isolation and the United Nations in assembly: it might be something like the "international system." More particularly, the norm-receivers would be those unnamed states that are seen as not implementing the duties mentioned in the Charters, the assumptions being that if these duties are lived up to the rights will be implemented.

The basic point, however, would be that the norm-objects are not individual human beings. And this raises the problem well known from the discussion of NIEO: what is the relationship between the rights of states as defined in this important Charter and the basic needs of individuals? In other words, is there compatibility between the NIEO approach to states, as an effort to satisfy interests and create social justice among states in the international system, and the basic needs approach to individual human beings as an effort to satisfy needs and create social justice among human beings in the intranational system?[43] Is there compatibility, contradiction, even conflict? And in any case, how is that to be handled?

The answer might be that the relationship is contingent. International social justice in the NIEO sense is neither a necessary nor a sufficient condition for intranational social justice in the basic needs sense. The two approaches may be about different things, at different levels. That it is not a necessary condition might be indicated by the circumstance that a range of basic needs has been met at least at the minimum level in many countries (South Korea, Taiwan, Sri Lanka, Kerala) without NIEO, as measured by physical quality of life indices.

To this it may be objected that for countries on top of the division of labor and privilege pyramid constituted by the old international economic order – roughly speaking the Western capitalist countries and some others – needs-satisfaction took place at the expense of other people's needs-satisfaction. Only by considering the total picture, analyzing the world as a system, can the incompatibility between the old international economic order and the basic needs approaches be clearly seen. To this, however, the answer might be that countries at lower levels of the old international economic order (such as Cuba) were nevertheless able to meet a range of basic needs, not by changing the international order, but by partly withdrawing from it and changing their intranational order in a revolutionary manner, giving a much higher priority, at least in some phases of the historical process, to ways of using the economic surplus in favor of basic needs-satisfaction for those most in need.

Thus, look at the socialist countries of the twentieth century. The People's Republic of China, for instance, did not wait for a new international economic order to meet the basic needs of what seem to have been very substantial portions of the population, leaving out others. But the objection may certainly be that basic material needs were then met at the expense of basic non-material needs, particularly freedom needs, and by following the general Western industrial models perhaps also at the expense of identity needs. It may be argued that only by considering the total range of needs can a clear picture of the total situation be obtained. To this it may then be countered that some needs are more basic than others. Only by looking at the process over time can judgements be arrived at. Not everything is possible at any given historical moment; and one has to start somewhere. These are now ex-socialist countries, perhaps emphasizing freedom needs at the expense of well-being needs.

The upshot of this argument would be that something like NIEO cannot be seen unambiguously as a necessary condition. And it is not a sufficient condition either, for the following reasons. The range of instruments considered in connection with NIEO as expressed in the Charter, and in the basic resolutions of the UN's 6th and 7th Special Assemblies, did not by themselves guarantee to the most deprived that they would become stronger people with a higher quality of life, material and non-material, for the most deprived in the countries supposed to benefit most from NIEO. That NIEO may be a sufficient basis for creating stronger *states* at the bottom of the present world hierarchy seems clear: a redistribution of capital resources will, for instance, make the militarily less powerful parts of the world system capable of acquiring more arms.

But NIEO or some similar new economic order can also be seen as a general strategy that is highly trade-orientated, trying to seek development through increased income from trade, which in turn would mean that efforts to use internal production factors for export will pay off more than in the past, among other reasons because of better and more stable terms of trade. The difficulty with this, however, is the reallocation of production factors for the production of exportable commodities rather than for subsistence products such as edible food stocks for the population. Thus, trade can be seen as a mechanism whereby the productive apparatus of society is channeled through some well defined, easily controlled gates such as harbors, airports, banking accounts, ministries of trade, etc., thereby increasing elite controls of the productive assets of a country.[44]

The rest, given this, becomes the question of what kind of elites the country has. Will they use their control powers to allocate a higher proportion of total resources in the country for the satisfaction of basic needs of the masses, or for building strong states, including the satisfaction of non-basic and sometimes even non-needs, of the elites? This should not be discussed in moral terms, using allegations of corruption, but rather in terms of what kind of structure the country has internally. Thus, if the socio-economic structure pumps the material surplus produced at the bottom up to the top, and the material surplus produced at the top (or coming in as positive trade balance, or current account surplus from the outside) remains at the top, then the linkage between NIEO and basic needs is not only weak but probably even negative.

In concrete terms this would mean that even under NIEO the surplus produced by the countless millions toiling under the sun, and in the sweatshops, for remuneration below the subsistence level of themselves and their families, will continue to do so. The fruits of their labor will be used to build strong states, not strong people. *And* the structure that could serve to redistribute wealth internally, such as free medication, free education, subsidized transport, better terms of exchange between goods produced in the countryside and goods produced in the cities, etc., will be absent, as under International Monetary Fund conditions. When there is little or no "trickling down" effect, but a well-functioning "pumping up" effect, the result is predictable: the country as a whole may undergo economic growth but the gap between the elites and the people will be increasing. Thus, NIEO is not a sufficient condition for needs-satisfaction. But some new international economic order, together with a new intranational economic order, might constitute a sufficient condition.[45]

The point we are aiming at is this: if needs should be used as an unquestionable guide in the construction of rights, then the "rights of states" package contained so far in the NIEO as a process should not have been accepted. But the world operates at several levels. Each level has its own logic, and it is legitimate to think and act in terms of rights of states and other collectivities (of which nations would be an important example), not only in terms of individuals. From the argument that NIEO is neither necessary nor sufficient to promote basic needs-satisaction does not follow that something like NIEO should not be implemented, and for a number of reasons.

First, what is not a necessary or sufficient condition today may be so tomorrow. Several scenarios might be envisaged, among them the possibility that a global redistribution of wealth that benefits only the top of the poorer societies will so much enrage the bottom that even the means of violent oppression accumulated through increased wealth are insufficient for the top to prevent major intranational transformations. The "IMF riots" over prices for food staples, accompanying the debt crisis, are good examples.

Second, increased resources may also open up channels of internal redistribution, so far unused because nothing or too little had been flowing through these channels. More money *may be* used for education and health services, not wasted on elite consumption or stacked away abroad. There is no guarantee they will be put to good uses, or that they will not.

Third, it is important to ask the question whether transforming the international economic order really serves basic needs. The contradictions should be pointed out. But the conclusions, today mainly negative, cannot stop that process; like asking whether the tidal waves around the world serve basic needs. They may or may not; in any case they *are*. In the same way there is a sense in which the dialectics of international economics simply *is*. A long-term political process, starting with Japan in 1868, breaking the Western monopoly on the world economy is taking place anyway, accelerating immediately after or during the Second World War (Iran 1951, Egypt 1956; Latin America). The mid-1970s UN instruments mentioned are only a minor part, a codification of some aspects of this process. And the present focus on "free trade" will not favor only the West, or mainly the West, even if they think so.[46]

Such instruments nevertheless play an important role. They may regulate the process, or at least the way of talking about the process. And there is also a closely related internal dialectic of the countries of the world. The art of politics in this context is to make use of both dialectics creatively, by exploring the conditions under which international economic justice and basic needs intranational justice can become compatible. One hint of a possible slogan in that direction: through self-reliance both at the local, national and regional levels.[47]

Finally, in addition to rights being operative at the system level, and at the level of collective actors, whereas needs are individually defined, rights may also be defined relative to the non-human environment. The right to a safe/clean/balanced environment does not as such express any one particular human need, but possibly addresses a cluster of material (health) and non-material (identity) needs.[48] Thus, the human need today for mammoths is probably low. But there is a high need for livelihood, for which an ecologically stable environment with a high level of biodiversity is a necessary condition.[49]

SOME WAYS IN WHICH RIGHTS MAY COUNTERACT NEEDS

Human needs are subtle. They are flexible, they vary in space and time, for instance in tune with the life-cycle of individuals. They are not easily understood and certainly not easily met. And as they are met, new needs tend to develop. In short: a very volatile concept. On the other hand, rights well institutionalized will tend to take on the rigidities of institutions, become inflexible, invariable, non-dialectical. In saying so a base is already laid for the discussion of some of the ways in which rights in fact might impede the satisfaction of needs.

Thus, the first and most important is probably the tendency for rights (given the present model with the United Nations as the supreme norm-sender, governments as norm-receivers and individuals, citizens, as norm-objects) to become universal. To this it may be objected that in the norm production process itself, involving the structurally and culturally very diverse governments and regions of the member states of the United Nations, there is a built-in guarantee against excessive universalism. Governments may protest, refuse to accept the outcomes of the norm production, in other words refuse to be senders of the norm. And, if that proves insufficient, they may refuse to receive the norm through non-ratification.[50]

However, the problem is that the government may not be able to articulate the needs of the population, or, in the case of authoritarian governments, may even suppress legitimate needs of the population. The human rights machinery crystallizes such contradictions by using cases of non-cooperation in norm production, or cases of non-ratification, as a way of rooting the norm more firmly.[51] Or, by having the population use the right as a basis for a claim in case the government has signed or ratified, something the government may have done in order to obtain other political or economic benefits that might offset the costs of not being able to redress popular grievances.[52] Thus, they might be seen as at least "generally cooperative."

These are relatively clear cases, however. What one should have in mind are more subtle needs than those usually considered in connection with "civil rights." Thus, in connection with schooling there is compatibility between the universal norm to provide for schooling, and the universal way in which schools are in fact built and used for educational purposes. But how sure are we that this corresponds to more basic needs lumped together under the heading of "education"? How much of what we associate with education is compatible with being taught from above? And how much is incompatible, based on searching alone and together with other students, to develop knowledge, rather than receiving knowledge?[53] In such images of the education process, very well known in all debates about education, schools may even stand in the way, and the whole process becomes less predictable from the point of view of governments.

Universalism in the sense of consensus among governments may be good for the power interests of governmental elites, but not for the educational needs of the people. In other words, the problem with universalism may be not so much international as intranational. The key problem is not whether consensus does or does not obtain among governments. The problem may very well be exactly that consensus is too easily obtained because of the shared interests all governments have in making their populations more disciplined and predictable. And the human rights formula is then applied to everybody, like shoes of size 40.

Similar considerations could apply to the problem of human rights over time. As countries evolve (on purpose we are not saying "develop"; that is more of a value judgement) the rights package to which they have subscribed may gradually become obsolete, responding less and less to the concrete situation. But countries can then subscribe to new rights, or at least new rights formulations. There will usually be something new available in storage, waiting for ratification, so that any country (meaning any government) can design its own trajectory through the human rights store. For that reason we should not worry so much about the number of ratifications for each human right, but, rather, focus on the human rights as an unfolding agenda, and how that agenda fits countries on different historical trajectories, and not only in different stages on the same trajectory. The task of the norm-producer is to make available a vast array of human rights programs, with a hard core that could be seen as more universal, expanding that core as civilizations learn through genuine dialogue to accept one another's rights.

However, the problem of time also enters at the level of individuals. Rights, like needs, tend to be formulated in a positive way. It might sound frivolous in a world of so much misery as ours even to mention a "need for hunger" as something accompanying a need for food. But there is nevertheless a deep reality behind that formulation. The "need for food" should probably be seen as shorthand for something much more complex: a need for oscillation between states of satisfaction and states of dissatisfaction where nutrition is concerned. It is hardly a need which is met by never feeling hunger, i.e. by continuously being fed, for instance intravenously. The satisfaction derived from food presupposes a state of hunger, which is not the same as moving into pathologies bordering on starvation. People may have very different rhythms for these oscillations between states of satisfaction and dissatisfaction. Perhaps the freedom to choose one's own rhythm is rather basic in connection with all types of need-satisfaction. Perhaps the process of needs-satisfaction, rather than the state of being satisfied, is what the need is about, a point which is rather obvious in connection with sexual gratification or with (other forms of) creative processes. The problem is whether the notion of rights can capture such more intricate notions at all, or whether the focus will be on one part only of the satisfaction–dissatisfaction continuum, thereby making what is highly dynamic highly static.

Then, there is the rather basic point that, in order to be productive of anything at all, rights have to be rather specific. If they are not, they are open to too many interpretations, and claims may then be rejected simply by citing an interpretation other than that of the claimant. But there is a limit to the extent needs can be specified without being distorted. Much of the discussion about needs has to do exactly with this: how far can we continue to subdivide needs without segmenting, atomizing something holistic, the human person as such?[54] Could it be that the whole construction of human beings as a "needs-package" is in itself a projection of certain atomizing, analytical features of Western epistemology, which in turn correspond to the high level of division of labor in Western societies, reflected in universities, in ministerial bureaucracies and in the (UN) agencies of international organizations? It is not difficult to imagine one ministry for each need, each of them the executors of the implementation of a corresponding human right, leaving sub-needs to subsections of the ministries, the whole thing reproduced at the international level in intergovernmental organizations in general, and in the United Nations family in particular. All of them embellished by the appropriate Ph.D.s from university departments. We have already gone quite far in this direction.

Human beings themselves are probably the best at putting it all together. If they are guaranteed survival, the basic constituents of economic well-being, identity, and freedom then they have a solid base from which they themselves can make a synthesis. If these things are not guaranteed, however, they will have more specific, more elementary worries. Knowing where the shoe pinches, they will build their lives around the needs deficits and not develop further.

The argument against this position, in turn, would be that no balanced rights package is in fact available, as the analysis in the preceding sections has indicated. Countries will pick some rights out of a total offering and filter others away, and in doing so they are steered less by a conception of the human needs of the population than by their conception of the power position of the country. The rights package will always be a distorted reflection of the needs package, and for that reason, when implemented, will also distort the total livelihood of human beings.

Thus, it is hardly a coincidence that rights are weak on identity at the same time as what might be interpreted as one of the major indicators of lack of identity, of alienation – mental disease – seems to be increasing throughout the Western industrialized world.[55] One solution might be to increase the norm production for the identity needs, possibly a future approach. The danger is, of course, that in the zealous effort to fill in the gaps too many rights will be constructed leading to overloading of the norm-receivers and under-loading of the norm-objects. And there is the added difficulty that even the most densely constructed rights package is exactly that, a *package* or a *set* or rights, not a holistic entity mirroring human beings in their entirety. In fact, the preceding sentence is mainly intuition; difficult to come to grips with, but a rather important intuition. The intuition is perhaps simply this: a need can be truly satisfied only in a context of other needs. The need never stands alone. And correspondingly for rights: the articles of the declarations and conventions subdivide what should be kept together. Thus, civil and political rights attain much more meaning when social and economic rights are satisfied, and vice versa.

Another obvious way in which rights may counteract needs is the division of labor in connection with the construction of rights. This has been pointed out above but bears repeating: participation in the *process* of producing norms is important, not only being a norm-object. In other words, to what extent does the process take care of "everyone's" need to be a norm-*subject* and a norm-*sender*, not only a norm-*object*? Participation of the population in formulating the norms would be a way of meeting a need to be the active master of one's own situation as opposed to being a client. This is hardly possible, except in a very diluted sense,[56] within the present (alpha) states/governments model: United Nations/states–governments/ citizens. It can only be possible at lower levels of social organization, for instance at the level of communities. The triad above could be supplemented by a compassion (beta) triad: people/people/people.

In a model of that type people themselves would work out the concrete content of the rights, and the task of higher levels of social organization would only be to steer that norm-production process in very general terms. *How* is a very problematic question, well known from the theory of federal structures. The division of labor in the production of human rights today is counterproductive from the point of view of the need to participate. The norm production that gave birth to the modern United States in 1776 and 1787, and to modern France in 1789, ran closer to the peoples than the inter-governmental committees two centuries later.

The major point in this connection, being made again and again in this chapter, is actually a special case of a much more general formula: how the human rights means supposed to serve the end of needs-satisfaction after some point tend to enter into a phase of rapidly decreasing utility, and then even into a region of rapidly increasing negative utility. The relation is somewhat as depicted in figure 3.2.[57] The broken straight line represents the optimistic assumption of "the more the better"; the curve a more realistic hypothesis.

In the future we may have to judge a country *negatively* by the number of human rights it has implemented, for instance because of the opportunity costs in terms of lost beta structures.[58] One of the ways in which this vertical division of labor becomes counterproductive is in the habit-forming tendency to look for higher levels of social organization as the solution to all kinds of problems. There is no denial of the tremendous potential and actual benefits to human beings from higher levels of organization, only a reminder of the

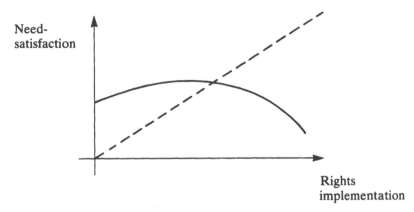

Figure 3.2   Relation between rights as means, and need-satisfaction as an end

opportunity cost involved: low levels will tend to be neglected and insufficiently expanded in depth to serve some of the same functions. The focus will be on problems as defined by higher levels, using the human rights package as an agenda even when low levels would have generated similar, but deeper agendas. In that way the human rights approach may not only meet needs but also create, artificially, new needs. Thus, freedom of expression interpreted at an individual level may make less sense in a more collectivist society; yet the propagation of human rights norms in that direction will tend to condition the population.

More serious, however, is the tendency of the human rights tradition to foster patterns of fragmentation and segmentation. The legal tradition will have a tendency to look for the guilty actor when a norm has been violated rather than looking for the wrong structure, as argued in the first section of chapter 2. The norm-receiver is an actor, and we are back to the problem of whether a structure can receive a norm.[59] The collective actor may have an inside structure, as is certainly the case for states. But the norm-receiver will ultimately have to be individuals responsible, or held to be responsible, for the collective actor; the "heads of states/governments," the "representatives." For this reason actor-dependent needs would generally be best covered by rights, as seen in the rich production of rights corresponding to freedom needs; and in the legal systems surrounding direct violence committed by individual and collective actors. The difficulty with rights applying to identity, for instance, is partly the problem of finding individuals personally responsible for acts that have alienation as a consequence. And correspondingly for rights applying to economic well-being: where are the actors responsible for misery? As with alienation they cannot usually be identified by intention, another cornerstone in legal paradigms.[60]

There is another approach. Instead of asking "who are guilty of misery and alienation?", which already sounds less meaningful than the corresponding question, "who are guilty of violence and repression?", one could ask: who are guilty of holding up actions that could lead to structural changes that would/might lead to higher levels of economic well-being and identity? Who stand in the way? The assumption would be that such actions have already been identified, that there is a high level of consensus about them and their consequences, and that they have been well communicated to the norm-receivers.[61] As will be explored later, this "acts of omission approach" may be useful in unpackaging wrong structures.

The human rights tradition might also have a fragmenting impact on the norm-objects. The rights, as opposed to the needs, tradition permits constructions in terms of collective actors. But today these actors are usually states, or nations, precisely because they have to be thought of as actors. There are many levels, often very loose, of social organization between these collective actors and the individual actors. Some of them are groups that on occasion act in concert; some of them (like corporations) are even "juridical persons." Others could more appropriately be referred to as social contexts. To take an example also used elsewhere in this text: a regime might claim that freedom of expression is implemented as long as individuals can be observed to express whatever they want. But the individuals might claim that the point is not only that they as individuals are permitted to express, but that others at the same time are permitted to be impressed by it. Speakers and writers presuppose a context of listeners or readers.

And this carries over into the point about segmentation. Rights have to be specific, and in so far as they are specific they will cover ever smaller segments of human action. The right to food may be implemented through a system of work-place canteens. But individuals may claim that it also matters with whom they eat (and where and when), not only that they eat and what they eat. This could be taken into consideration by a process of integrating rights; joining a right to food with a (non-trivial) right to togetherness with family members (commensalism). In principle this can be done, but it is quite clear that it has not been done to any significant extent so far. The main impression is one of segmentation, meaning that a structure of need-satisfaction satisfying one need here and now and with these people, and another need there and then and with those people, with no built-in right to integration, would be entirely compatible with the formulations of the rights. As expressed above: articles divide what broad concepts and philosophies unite. We need both.

We might summarize what has been said here by saying that the rights model, as pointed out in chapter 1, has built into it certain atomizing Western assumptions that may pass unnoticed in a Western or Westernized context, and that this will tend to twist and thwart need-satisfaction in a certain direction. With increasing consciousness this will become increasingly problematic for the human rights tradition as it is today.

POINTERS TO THE FUTURE: THE NEEDS/RIGHTS DIALECTIC

In figure 3.3 a needs/rights matrix has been prepared, with the 28 needs from the list in table 3.2 and the 49 rights (including sub-rights) in the Universal Declaration of Human Rights. This gives a total of 1,272 combinations. For 49 of them an indication of correspondence has been given. These figures, needless to say, are not very meaningful. Slight reformulations might change them. More interesting is the general shape of the matrix, bringing out an obvious point that nevertheless is worth repeating: the relationship is very far from one–one. There are rights that correspond to many, one and no needs; there are needs that correspond to many, one and no rights. And, as pointed out in the text, it ought to be like that. There are rights with no needs counterparts, which is not necessarily problematic. And there are needs with no rights counterparts. This may be problematic, but also a major source of renewal, serving as an invitation to continued norm-production; keeping the process as such alive.

As one outcome of this exercise let us now list, for the sake of easy overview, needs that might be considered important candidates on the world waiting list for processing into rights, as:

- the right to sleep
- the right to excretion
- the right not to be killed in a war, as civilian and as combatant
- the right not to kill in a war (conscientious objection)
- the right not to be exposed to excessively and unnecessarily heavy, degrading, dirty and boring work
- the right to be identified with one's own work-product, individually or collectively (as opposed to anonymity)
- the right of access to challenging work, requiring creativity
- the right to have control over the material surplus resulting from the work process
- the right to self-education and education with others (as opposed to schooling)
- the right to social transparency
- the right to co-existence with nature
- the right to be a member of some primary group (not necessarily the family)
- the right to be a member of some secondary group (not necessarily the nation)
- the right to be free to seek impressions from others (not only the media)
- the right to be free to experiment with alternative ways of life

If something like these were formulated as rights, figure 3.3 would look different. Most zeros at the foot would be eliminated, for instance. And the zeros to the right are no source of worry as long as other sources of rights validity can be found, such as social justice.

A list such as this may look naive, and the formulations not very precise. But that should not serve as an argument not to engage in an active needs/rights dialectic, even in the form of a dialogue between those more trained in thinking in terms of needs and those more trained in thinking in terms of rights. And that dialogue is also needed for well-rooted human rights in good standing simply because we have become too used to them. A fresh view is always useful. Human rights formulations have life cycles: there is conception and gestation before birth in a ceremonially accepted document. There is adolescence, maturity and senescence. No *formulation* is granted eternal life. But the underlying needs and rights may well be eternal, as long as human beings exist.

An interesting point for research would be the circumstances under which needs are translated into rights. One hypothesis might be: it does not depend on the solidity of the work done to justify the needs or the rights, but essentially on whether the dominant norm-senders are of the opinion that the new rights are already sufficiently

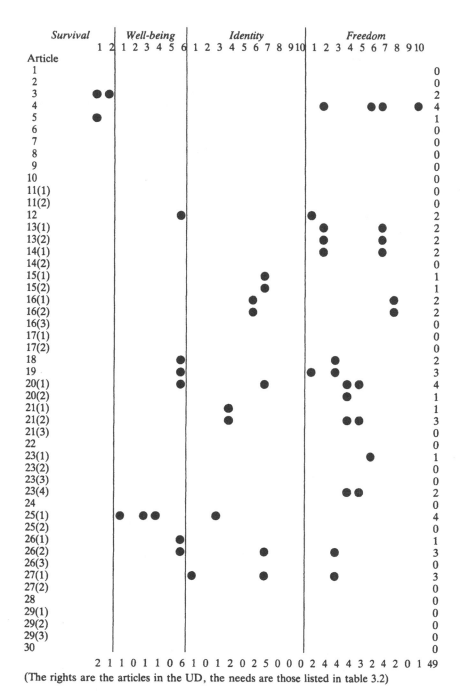

(The rights are the articles in the UD, the needs are those listed in table 3.2)

Figure 3.3 A needs/rights matrix (based on the Universal Declaration)

well implemented in their own countries. The new rights should not make dominant countries look bad and the others too good. Thus, an example we might have included in the list had it not been for the circumstance that we have abstained from social justice norms (they are too numerous, and in a sense too obvious) would have been: the right of old people to live with their families. This right is clearly directed against old-age homes. The likelihood that it would have been accepted by countries practicing large-scale removal of old people from their families and into old-age homes is negligible. A human right like that would put dominant countries of the First World far down the list where implementation is concerned. It might actually reverse the usual ranking, and would for that reason be resisted.

In this case, however, there is at least an understanding of what implementation would mean. For many of the other rights indicated above, decision-makers might not have any idea what implementation might mean, except for a vague feeling that it spells nothing good for their own countries. Everybody's right to creative work, for instance, is obviously in contradiction with the way modern, industrialized societies are organized, with creativity for few and routine work for many. Thus, if rights are accepted only when solutions are at hand, either we may have to wait for a long time or other groups would have to come into dominant positions as norm-senders.

Then, to change the perspective: is there any way in which the rights orientation might inspire the needs orientation; can the rights be used as a basis for defining new needs, for instance? Philosophically, theoretically yes, but in practice probably not. Those who do research on needs are considerably more free in probing the borderlines of the human condition than the rights people, tied as they are to institutional notions of negotiation, (near) consensus, and ratification. The dialogue would have to go in another direction: to instill in the needs people the idea that there are values other than those directly associated with individually experienced needs that should be accorded protection in the form of rights. This should by no means be interpreted to mean that with these two concepts the universe of discourse is closed. There is much more in the world in general, and in the world of development in particular, than needs + rights, for instance structures, power politics.

What, then, about the remaining category, the "things" that are on neither the list of needs nor the list of rights (see page 73). They are as important as anything on the two lists if either concept is to be dynamic, flexible and, one might add, chaotic, like the pattern in figure 3.3. Probably this category can best be strengthened or given life in a dialogue with people in general, outside the confines of the two kinds of "experts" alluded to above. Perhaps people in general see more clearly what is missing?

And that concludes this exploration of the needs/rights interface. The needs perspective has been used as an instrument of the human rights tradition. In the first chapter historical-structural and civilizational-cultural perspectives were used for the same purposes, to understand better the human rights tradition. And in the next chapters we shall turn to structure and process.

4

HUMAN RIGHTS AND SOCIAL STRUCTURES

HUMAN RIGHTS AND THE STRUCTURE OF DEVELOPMENT

Again we are faced with two extremely rich, complex and, above all, evolving concepts. This time "human rights" and "development"[1] are to be related to each other, and the agenda of the inquiry is, first, to look at the two ideas; second, to search for compatibilities and contradictions. A special warning against this kind of intellectual exercise should be given. Both concepts are evolving in concrete historical contexts, and will continue to do so. Consequently, there is a limit to how much can be obtained from a conceptual, logically orientated analysis. Typologies of "human rights" and "development" concepts can certainly be constructed and related to each other in the search for compatibilities and contradictions. This is useful, but the fact that both of them are parts of concrete historical processes must not be lost sight of. Thus, there may be some overriding compatibility due to belonging to the same broad historical process within the same culture and there may be some overriding contradictions built into exactly that process and because of mono-culturalism. In other words, what we find may say more about Western history and culture than about "development" and "rule of law" in general and "human rights" in particular.

As an example take the three sets of human rights discourses, sometimes called "generations": civil and political rights (CPRs); economic, social and cultural rights (ESCRs) and the possible rights to be, the solidarity rights (SRs). No doubt the first set is related to the interests of a bourgeoisie fighting its way out of feudal constraints; the second set to the interests of the working class and other groups marginalized and exploited, hurt and hit, by the emergence of that class as a dominant class; and the third set to the same kind of problems at the international level (development, peace and ecological balance), as an effort to overcome the contradictions created by international capitalism, private and state.

And the corresponding development concepts may be made to read like chapters in any book on Western history: the first set of development concepts is "blue" economic growth spearheaded by an entrepreneurial class unfettered by state control or initiative, guided by the *market*; the second set of development concepts is a reaction to this, "red" development – economic growth controlled, even initiated, by a state bureaucracy, but spearheaded by the labor movement, codified in a *plan*; and the third set of concepts is a reaction to both of the former, "green" development, based more on the autonomy of the local level and the presumed beauty of the smaller economic cycles, also for world solidarity, and spearheaded by the "new social movements." "Think globally, act locally," in other words.

Much of the current development debate is concerned with whether one first has to suffer the contradictions of the blue to become red; and then the contradictions of either or both, stemming from the circumstance that they both lead to big systems, in order to become green. As many poor, Third World countries still are to a large extent traditional green (as opposed to post-modern green), could they possibly be better off strengthening that social formation, building on top of it only a relatively weak blue and red sector? And could the rich, "first" and "second" world, blue and once red, countries have done better building down their entrepreneurial and bureaucratic giants, at the same time strengthening old and new types of local communities? The sympathies of the author are in this general direction. But what happens right now seems to be red turning blue and blue turning even more blue, with more giantism ("globalization") and more giant problems, with green opposition building up all over the world, and brown/black fascist frustration with the blue, yet anti-green, around the corner.

So both human rights and development concepts have their roots in, and are reflections of, Western history. It belongs to the picture that the West has a tendency to assume that Western history = universal history (see the opening section of chapter 1), meaning that not only human rights concepts but also development concepts are abstracted from Western history, universalized and exported to the rest of the world under the guise of "modernization."

This ultra-brief excursion into the history of development/ development of history brings out two key dimensions in development theory and practice, namely:

1 *Level*: is it predominantly *macro-orientated*, building strong countries (with strong entrepreneurial and/or bureaucratic elites) and an international order accommodating the power and privileges of these interest elites, *or* is it predominantly *micro-orientated*, building strong human beings and strong local communities (or basic autonomous units in general) in which human beings can unfold themselves *à l'hauteur de l'homme*?

2 *Aspect*: is it predominantly *one-dimensional*, and in that case does it focus on economic dimensions, on social structure, on institution-building, on ecological dimensions, on cultural aspects, or what else, *or* is there an attempt to be *multi-dimensional*, even "holistic," taking the "totality" as the focus of development, encompassing a number of dimensions?

This gives us four styles of development; and there can be little doubt that so far what we have seen is mainly the "macro-orientated, one-dimensional economic" combination. There have been two basic models, liberal-capitalist and the marxist-socialist, both focusing on the economic dimension in its blue and red varieties, the former leading to growth without much control, the latter to control without much growth, exemplified by the two superpowers of the Cold War. The crisis (with few exceptions) of these two models, when exported to the Third World, is known today as the "development crisis." Exacerbating the situation has been the fact that the two superpowers used to demand of their client states that they by and large adhere to the blue and red development models respectively. If not, they were branded as security risks. Today this has changed drastically in the former red camp but not in the blue. That change is still to come.

At the other extreme, then, is the multi-dimensional, micro-orientated approach, often called "human development" and "community development." This approach was very popular in the early decades of post-Second World War development practice. Characteristic of most theories and some practice in this tradition is a high level of local self-reliance, short economic cycles, informal/ green economies, direct democracy, much participation, and much emphasis on human growth and personal development through health services and education. Many such communities, however, tend to focus on only one such aspect and hence become very imbalanced. And many countries, of course, focus not only on the economy but also on very much else (often called social development) and then become more balanced. All four combinations can be found empirically, but with a prevalence of the two mentioned.

Which is the "correct" style of development? One possible answer would be to say "all of them," the answer preferred by the present author. However, as the current processes are so overwhelmingly of the macro-orientated, one-dimensional type a strong emphasis on the opposite type is needed today, not an exclusively green, but a green*er* approach, to obtain better balance. Real quality of life can probably best be experienced and obtained at the micro level. But the macro level is a rather strong reality and can both facilitate and impede this local quality of life dramatically. Moreover, we may praise holism, but total thinking and total practice may lead to inaction since everything becomes too complicated to make any first move, or to totalitarianism since everything has to be changed at once. The latter may not be so dangerous if only one small community is involved. But as a blueprint for a whole country, or for *all* communities, it can become very dangerous. Hence, starting in one corner, with one aspect, even introducing contradictions between the "old" and the "new" to get a process going, with much richer totalities in mind, may not be the worst approach. After all, imbalance can also have a very energizing impact to rectify the imbalance.

The *basic needs* approach is crucial as a guide in any development process. It is a protest movement: do not forget the human level; in all the efforts to build strong countries do not forget the purpose of it all, building strong human beings! The developmentalists of the blue and red varieties tried to co-opt the human needs movement by making it one-dimensional, focusing on the material human needs most clearly related to their economic growth and institution-building. Precisely because of their success, e.g. in the UN organizations of the 1960s, 1970s and 1980s, dominated by the blue and the red together, micro-level development becomes even more important today to correct the course. But it has to cater to all kinds of human needs, material and non-material. No doubt, if the green movement with its anarchist overtones of "small is beautiful," mindless of the extent to which "some big is necessary," were really successful there would be scope for a protest movement in favor of more macro-orientated approaches. Today the macro movements are more than sufficiently "successful," and very deeply entrenched. No reason for that worry, so far.

Thus, development is seen as a complex dialectic between the micro and macro levels, and between the one-dimensional and the more holistic approaches. Where, then, do the human rights fit into all of this?

Basic human rights share with basic human needs a universal concern for everybody, not only for the needs of the strong and the rights of the privileged. Precisely for that reason first priority should be for the needs of the most needy and the rights of those whose basic human rights have been most violated. In principle these are approaches from the bottom up, an indispensable corrective to the top-heaviness and the self-serving nature of so much of what elites put forward as "development." But human rights differ from human needs in being institutionalized in the particular tripartite way described in the first part of chapter 1, linking a *norm-sender* (principally the UN General Assembly), *norm-receivers* (the governments duty-bound to implement the norm), the *norm-objects* (the holders of the right, usually the individuals), and then there is also the *norm-content* (the substantive content of the norm).

Thus, there is little doubt that by its very structure the three-tier human rights tradition is more consonant with top-heavy, blue-red development protected, facilitated or initiated by the state, and less with development based on small, basic and autonomous units where the primordial beta-channel human rights tradition, the mutual rights and obligations, would fit better. Thus, there is the implicit stand pointed out in chapter 3: the human rights tradition is an alpha-channel, macro approach coming to the rescue of the micro level, and in so doing increasing the legitimacy of the UN General Assembly, and the governments of states, at the expense of making the micro level more dependent. As rights multiply so would, or should, the machineries to make them really justiciable: detection and reporting processes, adjudication processes, sanction processes, review processes. The more macro the system the more complex the machineries to make the rulers accountable to their subjects. And vice versa; the more complex the machineries, the more macro the system.

None of this should be considered more than warnings. As long as the basic human rights work in the interests of the most deprived the tradition is invaluable even if there are certain built-in limits to growth and dangers down the road. But it raises the question: could something between the codified, top-heavy human rights and the uncodified, bottom-level mutual rights and obligations be more compatible with green development, and hence something that *in the present phase of human history* should be encouraged? More explicit, more codified, but also more left to local processes of accountability, breaking the age-old tradition that the more terrible the crime, and the higher the status of the actors, the "higher" the level of the court till one ends up at the governmental and intergovernmental, supreme court and International Court of Justice levels, thereby sanctifying those levels?

Of course, there are very good reasons for this. If in the present phase of human history, nation state building and international architecture with states as building blocks are the orders of the day, and most big crimes are committed by big governments and major corporations, then something is needed high up for adjudication. This becomes particularly important in the field of solidarity rights. But the institutions leave the local communities practically speaking without a say. They are sidetracked from the very beginning, with little or no human rights or development, except as objects, or institution-building. Had it not been for Amnesty International the system would not have worked at all. By working locally they also become local norm-senders to local norm-receivers (prison wardens, police officers); making the norms more meaningful.

What we are looking for is the consistent translation of human rights thinking into local normative culture, but then emphasizing the basic needs entitlement rather than the universality found, for instance, in the four components of the International Bill of Human Rights. Particular human rights, made specific to local culture and historical context, may be as significant as universal human rights. But one approach does not exclude the other. Both–and, not either–or.

Let us then turn to another dimension of human rights thinking of basic significance for the right to development, picking up the train of thought from the opening section of chapter 2: is the right institution- or structure-orientated? The meaning of this crucial distinction can be seen from a couple of examples:

In the field of food:	Is the focus on being fed, or on living in a structure able to produce sufficient food through the appropriate structural arrangements?
In the field of health:	Is the focus on access to institutions for somatic and mental health service, or on living in a structure that produces a maximum of somatic and mental health?
In the field of energy:	Is the focus on having access to energy conveniently converted, or on living in a structure able to obtain energy conversion?
In the field of participation:	Is the focus on access to a ballot box or on life in a participatory structure?

In the following sections some indications will be given of what the structural approach in the fields of food, energy and health might mean concretely. The key point would be local self-reliance, even to the point of local self-sufficiency, where these three fundamentals are concerned. "Local" does not necessarily mean the small community. It could also mean bigger units if the economic geography makes self-reliance at the truly local level impossible. With some important technological innovations in recent years, especially in the field of energy conversion, there should be room for some optimism in this field.

In the "structural approach" the basic idea is that certain goods and services are made available at a high level of *automaticity*, and that certain bads and disservices (such as famine, disease, pollution, and depletion) are avoided, also at a high level of automaticity. Example: pollution/depletion control is built into the structure when a farmer growing foodstuffs for subsistence is eco-conscious because he knows that he and his offspring will be the victims of the consequences of eco-imbalances. The transnational agro-business corporation does not have to take this into account as the consequences will be far away, and when they become too disastrous the TNC will, like nomads but less softly, move to other areas on which to prey. In the structural approach certain obstacles are removed by changing the structure. The approach is preventive rather than curative, like exercise and a healthy diet when the focus is on bads and disservices. Obviously they do not exclude each other.

All of this can also be obtained at the macro level, nationally and internationally, by governments and by intergovernmental organizations, but is more decision-dependent, less automatic. And there is one thing that cannot be obtained at the macro level: direct participation, a collectivity small enough to permit not only identification but direct participation so as to trigger off the mechanisms that ensure the automaticity, not only benign action from above, but the accumulated effect of myriads of actions below. The structural approach has as a condition at least an element of smallness. We say an "element," for those small communities could, of course, also be parts of something bigger, such as a confederation of basic social units, based both on the solidarity within and the solidarity among such communities. The key word is actually *solidarity*, and the key problem is how one builds a structure where solidarity is automatic.

Again, it is obvious that the thrust of the human rights approach has been at the macro rather than at the micro level, and institutional rather than structural. The first distinction reflects the personal interests of many people behind the human rights approach, more attracted by the glory of the macro level, governmental and/or intergovernmental, than the anonymity of the local level. The second distinction reflects their deep ideology, more actor-orientated than structure-orientated, and hence more geared towards institution-building than structural transformation. These people themselves will either deny the former, or deny that it has any significance other than positive; and they would be blind to the significance of the latter, seeing, like everybody, better the biases of others than of themselves.

So, what then is *the* relationship between "development" and "human rights?" In a sense all that has been said above: a question both of compatibility and contradiction; of compatibility with blue/red development and contradiction with the green approaches. But from that it does not follow that the only valid approach is micro-level, holistic development, protected by building adequate structures that define mutual rights and obligations. This would first of all presuppose a world where all societies are in the same historical situation (avoiding "stage" or any such term); and, second, that the good society is the contradiction-free society. Of the two sets of four approaches, one for development and one for human rights, there is no reason to be in total disfavor of any of them, or of any of the combinations. The richness and complexity of these schemes bear some testimony to the richness and complexity of the human condition in general. But having said that, there is little doubt that much more emphasis should be placed on local level approaches both for development and for human rights, and on the structural approaches for both of them.

FOOD, HEALTH AND ENERGY

From the general reflections in the preceding section some specific focusing on the right to development in such fields as food, health and energy should flow relatively easily.[2] What is needed is a clear image of the *goals* of food, health and energy development so that we know better what rights in these fields are supposed to protect or promote. In doing this we can be guided by the discussion above, emphasizing structure and automaticity. The right to development has also to be very closely related to human needs. But they are complex, as indicated in chapter 3, comprising at the very minimum the broad classes of needs for survival, well-being, identity, and freedom. Then, a warning: a structural approach always takes place in a context. The right to *development* would also place certain demands on the developmental context. Production and distribution to satisfy needs are necessary but not sufficient. Respect for nature, structure and culture are also matters of deep significance.

Food

Let us first try for the "field of food," knowing in advance that this is a misleading formulation. The whole idea of a holistic approach to development is precisely that there is no such thing as the "field of food" in isolation. It is not a sector; but certainly an aspect of the development discourse. And that discourse demands that we run through the whole gamut of goals of development to identify the food aspect of each one of them.

1   *Survival*, meaning the probability that one will not die from starvation, whether that starvation is brought about by misguided production, wrong distribution, ecological imbalances, lack of self-reliance, including dependency on those who can make use of "food as a weapon," for instance in connection with economic

sanctions. Basically this is a question of *sustainability*, over time, e.g. over seasonal variations of the food supply.

2 *Well-being*, meaning quantitatively and qualitatively adequate food consumption; at the individual level. There is a *subjective* approach, the individual human being's own judgement, and an *objective* approach, a "scientific" approach which in turn would split into Western ethno-science (which Westerners call "science") and non-Western ethno-sciences. Table 4.1 suggests possibilities. Nothing less than the complete set of these possibilities should be considered. To disregard the individual's own judgement is professional arrogance; to disregard non-Western approaches is Western arrogance and parochialism. Both are widespread.

Table 4.1 Food development goals

Approach	Quantitative	Qualitative
Subjective	Feeling of a full stomach; no hunger pain	Eating something that tastes good
Objective (Western)	Adequate amount of calories, proteins, vitamins, etc.	Adequate balance, harmony
Objective (non-Western)	Adequate amount relative to need	Adequate balance, yin/yang, cold/hot, etc.

3 *Identity*, meaning whether the production and consumption of food engender contact with Self, Others, society, culture, and nature and not only something remote and external with total alienation between producers, distributors, and consumers.

4 *Freedom*, meaning the possibility of choice, and consciousness about the consequences of the choice, both with regard to production and consumption of the food – including the possibility of choosing (but as an act of free will) status quo in production and consumption.

5 *Production*, meaning whether factors/inputs in necessary and sufficient quantity and quality are available for producing foodstuffs to bring about 1, 2, 3, and 4.

6 *Distribution*, meaning whether the level of satisfaction from participation in consumption *and* production for those at the bottom in terms of 1, 2, 3, and 4 is increasing, and more particularly so that discrepancies in satisfaction level for the total population and between groups are decreasing. The floor has to be raised; the ceiling may have to be lowered and waste avoided. Key special cases: equality of genders in food production and consumption, and children survival.

7 *Nature*, meaning that the level of maturity of the eco-system, both in terms of diversity and symbiosis, is increasing or at least not decreasing as a result of food production/consumption – as a necessary condition for securing the food basis for future generations. Bio-organic approaches are one response to this demand.

8 *Structure*, meaning that food-related needs are satisfied to a large extent on a local basis and that there is a potential for local adequacy, even in cities, in times of crises (food autarchy when necessary), including seasonal variations, thereby decreasing the possibility of using food as a weapon.

9 *Culture*, meaning that the food system used strengthens the viable cultural patterns and is not a vehicle of unwanted penetration of another culture expressing other values and tastes, and engendering unwanted relations to others and to nature (unless, of course, this is the outcome of a conscious, voluntary, participatory choice).

The totality of this, then, is the deeper goal of food development. However, the ultimate unit of development in this perspective is the individual human being as only individuals can sense deprivation and satisfaction of food needs.

Health

Let us then try the same for the "field of health," again knowing in advance that this is a misleading formulation. The whole idea of a holistic approach to development is precisely that there is no such thing as the "field of health," taken in isolation. It is not a "sector." It may be said to be an *aspect* of the development discourse, however. And that discourse now requires of us that we, once again, run through the whole gamut of goals of development to identify the health aspect of each one of them.

1 *Survival*, meaning the probability that one will not die from a disease prematurely, whether that premature death is brought about by misguided health care, wrong distribution, ecological imbalances, lack of self-reliance (including dependence on those who can make use of "health as a weapon" by withholding health inputs). Fundamentally, this is a question of *sustainability* over time, e.g. across natural and social hazards (violence), of basic health inputs.

2 *Well-being*, meaning a state of somatic and mental well-being, "health" at the individual level. There is a subjective approach, the individual's own judgement, and an objective approach, a "scientific" approach which in turn would split into Western ethno-science and non-Western ethno-sciences. In addition there is a distinction between negative health (absence of morbidity) and positive health (e.g. capacity for love and creative work, not to be trivialized as capacity for sex and performance in a job). Table 4.2 suggests possibilities. A major part of this table is

Table 4.2 Health development goals

Approach	Negative health	Positive health
Subjective	No pain, no suffering	A positive sense of vitality
Objective (Western)	Symptom-free	
Objective (non-Western)	Symptom-free	Balance, harmony, elements, liquids, yin/yang

empty: there is no consensus about indicators of positive health in the Western approach. Nothing less than the complete set of these possibilities should be considered. To disregard the individual's own judgement is professional arrogance; to disregard non-Western approaches is Western arrogance. Both are widespread.

3 *Identity*, meaning that the production and consumption of health inputs by Self, by Others, by professionals, in the Western and in the non-Western sense (Ayurvedic, acupuncture, shaman) will provide for some contact with Self, Others, society, culture and

nature and not be something remote and external, with total alienation between the producers and consumers of health.

4 *Freedom*, meaning the possibility of choice, and consciousness about the consequences of choice, with regard to both production and consumption of health inputs – inviting people to design their own health–illness–health cycles (under some "mild guidance"), e.g. entirely Western, entirely non-Western or mixed.

5 *Production*, meaning whether factors/inputs in necessary and sufficient quantity and quality are available for producing health inputs to bring about 1, 2, 3, and 4.

6 *Distribution*, meaning whether the level of satisfaction from participation in consumption *and* production for those at the bottom in terms of 1, 2, 3, and 4 is increasing, and more particularly so that discrepancies in health level for the total population and between groups are decreasing. The floor has to be raised; the ceiling may have to be lowered. Key special cases: equality of genders in health matters, children survival.

7 *Nature*, meaning that forms of co-existence with nature are found more conducive to human health. This probably involves much deeper (not higher) levels of insight into nature's ways than known today when our approach to vectors of contagious disease is only "seek and destroy" combined with inoculation, and our approach to earthquakes and hurricanes/*tsunamis*, etc. is even less than that.

8 *Structure*, meaning that health-related needs are satisfied to a large extent on a local basis and that there is a potential for local adequacy in times of crises (health autarchy when necessary) – thereby decreasing the possibility of using health as a weapon, including in economic sanctions.

9 *Culture*, meaning that the health system used strengthens the viable cultural patterns and is not a vehicle of unwanted dominance by another culture, expressing other values and tastes, and engendering unwanted relationships to others and to nature (unless, of course, this is the outcome of a conscious, participatory choice).

The totality of this, then, is the deeper goal of health development. However, the ultimate unit of development in this perspective is the individual human being as only individuals can sense deprivation and satisfaction of health.

Energy

Finally, let us try the field of "energy," again knowing that this is a misleading formulation. The whole idea of a holistic approach to development is precisely that there is no such thing as "the field of energy" taken in isolation. Again, it is not a "sector;" but certainly an *aspect* of the development discourse. And that discourse requires that we run through the whole gamut of goals of development to identify the energy aspect of each one of them.

It should perhaps be added at the very beginning that this ninefold approach to energy (like that for food and health, above) is not conceived of here as an ideological position, but as a minimum checklist. It is well known that the conventional engineering position is based on scientific technological feasibility (and here the border-lines are pushed further and further out due to scientific research) combined with commerical profitability, and that some concerns for ecological factors have recently been added to this short-list. The claim is that the list of concerns has to be much longer, and that those who curtail that list and end up with such small lists as just mentioned should be seen as poor intellectuals in addition to being propagators of certain value positions. The proof of lack of quality lies in the present human energy predicament.

1 *Survival*, meaning the probability that there will be a *sustainable* energy supply at least at a minimum level, across seasonal variations and international conjunctures. Thus, it means independence of those who can make use of "energy as a weapon," by having regionally, nationally, locally, to some extent even down to the individual household, an invulnerable minimum energy supply. But survival also means that energy cycles are constructed in such a way that massive destruction cannot be caused through breakdowns along the cycles, such as explosions in nuclear reactors, with consequent fallout (Three Mile Island, Chernobyl). Such considerations certainly also apply to more classical energy cycles; the many deaths suffered by miners in coalmines are examples of violence in energy production. In this connection the cynical comparison (made by people with a very low level of empathy with workers?) of the possible numbers of victims from nuclear catastrophes versus coalmining should be

strongly rejected. One of the conclusions to be derived from such data should be to make coalmines more secure, not morally bankrupt comparisons. Furthermore, energy cycles should be constructed in such a way that they do not invite sabotage or terrorism, nor attract missiles and attack in general because there are nodes on the energy cycles that when knocked out could cause major breakdowns in the total social system. In short, *survival is seen here basically as a question of invulnerability to internal and external forces of the energy conversion processes.*

2 *Well-being*, meaning that the minimum energy supply for the satisfaction of basic material needs is guaranteed. There are energy inputs for the production of food, for housing (although the heating factor can be considerably reduced through insulation, without reducing the "material comfort"), for the production of health and education inputs, for transport and communication and, indeed, for the creation of labor-saving devices that can liberate human beings from work that is unnecessarily heavy, degrading, dirty and/or boring.

In other words, it is fully recognized that there is a need for "comfort." This need *can* be over-satisfied and *is* over-satisfied in over-developed countries by eliminating too many kinds of manual forms of energy, with obesity as a consequence. Such considerations will have to enter the entire thinking about energy. If energy cycles (from extraction of energy resources to conversion of energy, through distribution to its end use) are constructed in such a way that along the cycle people develop "modernization diseases" (tumors, cardiovascular diseases, mental disorder) in ways that can be shown to be related to the energy cycle then obviously something has gone wrong. Failure to include such considerations in thinking about energy is intellectually dishonest.

In short, the basic leading question in connection with energy cycles would be whether they are sufficient to satisfy basic human needs for the entire population, and do not counteract basic human needs for some or even most. Thinking about energy should start from this point, not from technological feasibility and/or commercial validity and/or administrative convenience, the typical considerations of researchers, capitalists and bureaucrats.

If we now make a distinction between energy for basic needs and energy for non-basic wants (some of which are rather extravagant, such as military races, space expeditions, electric toothbrushes) on the one hand, and on the other hand a distinction between soft and hard energy cycles, we arrive at table 4.3. The soft energy cycles are defined as satisfying the nine

Table 4.3 A typology of energy conversion processes

Energy cycles	Energy for basic needs	Energy for non-basic wants
Soft	"Traditional" farming	For art, culture
Hard	Modern farming	For "modern" consumption

demands in this list; the less they are satisfied the harder the energy cycle.

Any energy budget should be disaggregated in such a way that it is shown clearly how much is used for basic needs and how much for extravagant wants. Moreover, a society's capacity for generating energy the soft and the hard ways should be examined, and *the general hypothesis would be that soft energy cycles by and large would be sufficient to cover our basic needs.* The demand for hard energy cycles is tied to extravagant wants, among them also aggressive export policies substituting for local production for basic needs.

This is not the same as saying that all energy should derive from soft energy cycles and should be only for basic needs. This is not an argument for a bare minimum, frugal world. It is essentially an argument in favor of seeing clearly where we stand, what the true energy situation is. And it may one day be important: one day a World Energy Authority might have to come into being to distribute energy resources more equitably. One way to obtain fair distribution would be by asking whether the end use is for basic needs or for extravagant wants, giving considerably lower priority to the latter. Any authority with a regulatory function of that type would lead to a reduction of energy conversion in high-income countries and an increase in low-income countries. It should also be noted that among the "soft energy cycles" are nature's own cycles that supply by far the greater part of our energy. Many of the arguments are in favor of "helping nature a little," building on the two major miracles surrounding us: the inflow of inexhaustible solar energy, and photosynthesis. The bio-mass converter is a good example.

3 *Identity*, meaning that the conversion and end use of energy inputs by Self, Others, and professionals would provide for *contact* with Self, Others, society, culture, nature and not be something remote, external, alienating. Above all, it should be entirely comprehensible. Energy cycles should be transparent, understandable so that citizens know what is going on, can act upon them in order to forestall bad, one-sided policies, and also know how to react in crisis, when the system breaks down.

4 *Freedom*, meaning the possibility of choice, of having a grid of energy cycles to choose from, and to be in a position to compose one's own energy cycle profile at the household, local, national, regional level. As usual freedom should not reduce the freedom of others, already putting severe constraints on the possibility of opting for hard energy cycles. It should also be noted that by using hard energy technologies one cannot have both security and freedom. If the most vulnerable points in a hard energy technology cycle are to be adequately "protected" against sabotage, terrorism, enemy attack, explosions, the result is likely to be a police state. The battles over which energy path to be chosen already indicate the close linkage between hard energy cycles and threats to civil liberties, meaning human rights.

5 *Production*, meaning whether factors/inputs in necessary and sufficient quantity and quality are used for producing energy inputs so as to bring about 1, 2, 3, and 4. In this connection special attention should be paid to the energy used to "produce" energy; often a substantial proportion of the total energy conversion. Thus, total and honest budgets for energy conversion cycles have to be produced.

6 *Distribution*, meaning whether the level of satisfaction from using energy for those at the bottom of society, in terms of 1, 2, 3, and 4 is increasing, and more particularly so that discrepancies in satisfaction level for the total population and between groups are decreasing. The floor has to be raised; the ceiling in energy conversion has to be lowered in order to bring about a higher level of equality and social justice in energy end use. Special attention has to be paid to the heavy energy losses incurred when hard energy cycles are operating over long distances.

7 *Nature*, meaning that energy resources are destroyed because they are non-renewable, or that wastes from energy "production" and consumption may be toxic. More particularly it means that nature's diversity and homeostatic mechanisms are not impaired by the energy cycles. And even more particularly, more directly related to the energy aspect, it means that the quality of the energy, the negentropy, is maintained.

8 *Structure*, meaning that energy demands to a large extent are satisfied on a local basis and that there is a potential for local adequacy in times of crisis (energy autarchy when necessary), thereby decreasing the possibility of using energy as a weapon. It should be noted that a centralized energy supply system will make villages and isolated households highly vulnerable to centralized decisions by people who might threaten to cut off the energy supply if the periphery becomes recalcitrant. The same applies internationally. Economic sanctions are based on energy self-insufficiency.

9 *Culture*, meaning that the energy system used strengthens the viable cultural patterns and is not a vehicle of unwanted dominance of another culture, expressing other values and tastes and engendering other relations to others and to nature (unless, of course, this is the outcome of a conscious, participatory choice).

The totality of this, then, is the deeper goal of energy development. The indicators will tell us where we stand at a given place, at a given point in time. However, the ultimate unit of development in this perspective is the individual human being, as only individuals can sense deprivation and satisfaction of needs.

Conclusion

What is at stake in all three cases is a total structure, not merely food, health and energy provided by "somebody" (meaning market or plan, both vulnerable). Evidently this is a deeper human right than the shallow human right to food, health and energy, regardless of how provided. In defense of the "shallow" human right there is the argument that what matters is food, health and energy here and now, and how. But that is exactly the point: this is as far as that kind of human rights tradition brings us. In principle a well-organized prison would do. Other human rights serve as guarantees against societies organized as prisons. But where are the rights guaranteeing a deeper development?

ON THE RIGHT TO MENTAL HEALTH

To make the points in the preceding subsections more clear, let us try them out in a particularly sensitive and less materialistic field, mental health, to see where the institutional and the structural approaches carry us. The basic problem can be reformulated as follows: on the one hand there is the human rights tradition, on the other the tragic phenomenon of soaring mental disorders, so indicative of alienation, of loss of identity. How do the two relate to each other? Is it like a well-coupled set of cog-wheels so that when the human rights machinery is put into motion and engaged (as in an automobile) with the mental health phenomena, the negative trends will be reversed? Or could it be that this would accelerate them further? Or are the two machineries permanently disengaged, and simply irrelevant to each other?

To explore this some perspective on mental disorder phenomena is indispensable. Much is known about the social distribution of mental disorders, although certainly not enough. Thus, in general it seems clear that they belong, with some exceptions, to the category of "human-made" rather than "nature-made" diseases, granted that human-made causes may work through physiological factors. A warning, however, should be issued against taking that dichotomy too literally: they obviously interact. Only few nature-made phenomena would hit everybody equally. An earthquake tends to kill more dwellers in poorly made than in more solid houses, a *tsunami* hits poor fishermen close to the coastline more than others, etc. Mental disorder is particularly prevalent in urban lower classes and among the old, possibly because of disruption of family ties and primary groups in general. On the other hand, mental disorder also seems to accompany economic growth. Many forms seem to be more prevalent after than before the industrial revolution and more in the "developed" (capitalist or socialist) countries than in the "developing" world. For that reason mental disorder is often included in the list of "modernization diseases," together with malignant tumors and cardiovascular diseases. The obvious prediction is that those parts of Third World countries that "catch up" with the industrialized West, e.g. Singapore (and the other three "mini-Japans/Chinas": Hong

Kong, Taiwan, South Korea), Tehran, Nairobi, Sao Paulo, and Mexico City, will suffer the same consequences, although it will take some time before the rates reach Manhattan, NY proportions.

Given this, how can we understand mental disorder? Epistemologically a multi-level, multi-disciplinary approach will serve, as for cancer. No single-minded focus on "virus," blaming it all on "nature," in the Judeo-Christian tradition often seen as the enemy of "humanity," beastly, to be conquered by "search and destroy," will do. To the extent that mental disorder is socio-culturally induced the following formulation should capture a good portion of the variance:[3]

Mental disorder will occur as a result of the concurrence of:

1   a strengthening of large, vertical alpha structures;
2   a weakening of small, horizontal beta structures protecting individuals;
3   the diffusion of a "promethian," individualist, competitive ethos.

Thus, the phenomenon is here seen essentially as due to the diffusion of a certain combination of structural and cultural processes, the modernization syndrome. Individuals become absorbed into large structures, vertical, penetrating and segmenting, fragmenting and marginalizing, built by bureaucracies and/or corporations, inside which fight, struggle and (regulated) competition rather than cooperation, mutual aid and support would be the rule. Another word for this type of process is "Westernization," and still another (a misnomer) is "development." That this particular structural/cultural combination is capable of producing economic growth is well known. But it also produces economic disparities. And the hypothesis here also relates it to mental breakdown. Perhaps it may simply be said that human beings are not made for that type of structure; that we need a higher level of togetherness than offered by the "alpha strong"/"beta weak" combination. Hence the thesis would *not* be the facile statement that "growth in mental disorder is due to economic growth." Rather, both of them can be seen as concomitant manifestations of a more deeply rooted structural/cultural phenomenon (note that the word "cause" is not used in this sentence).

How, then, can the human rights tradition enter the field of mental health? Broadly speaking, there seem to be two possible answers to this question, as indicated in the preceding section: a shallow approach, and a deep approach. The terms "shallow" and "deep" are not intended to reflect on the intellectual level, or the ethical devotion, of the proponents, but on the location of the phenomena they address themselves to.

The shallow approach is the institutional "access to services" approach, perhaps best available to upper- and middle-class intellectuals in Manhattan, a setting saturated with psychotherapists of various persuasions. Ultimately the right to mental health would be interpreted as a claim on governments to make psychiatric hospitals, psychiatrists, tranquilizers, etc. more widely available, seeing to it that they are covered by social security schemes. There is some evidence to indicate that most of these "services" may exacerbate the phenomena further, among other reasons because mental hospitals are much richer in alpha than beta structures (except for the defensive beta structures the patients manage to make themselves, *vide* the movie *One Flew Over the Cuckoo's Nest*). It should also be noted how the entire institutional approach invariably will produce more alpha structure and less beta structure, more dependence on states and corporations (ministries of health and pharmaceutical firms), less on family and friends. It will therefore be favored by those bent on strengthening these organizations.

The deep approach would look at the structural and cultural causes, and challenge the whole Westernization/modernization/development syndrome; a task Westerners, modernizers and developers would generally not be good at. They would tend to identify "problems," and create one specialty, one discipline, potentially also one human rights package around each, leaving the basic phenomena unchallenged. The alternative ways of life movements in rich countries can be seen as an effort to come to grips with this, building a social environment where alpha structures are weaker and informal beta structures stronger, and the whole ethos less competitive and individualizing. The legal paradigm will in general not capture such phenomena at all since there is no concrete juridical person to whom claims may be addressed. There is no individual intention or guilt to hitch on to, no unlawful acts of commission or omission, nobody who can be arraigned in court. It is difficult (as argued in chapter 2) to put structures and cultures into courts.

Or is this not necessarily the case? Could the human rights tradition nevertheless be used to promote a more structural approach?

The prediction above is certainly that the "access to services" (nobody should be more than X km away from a primary psychiatric health service, with a licensed psychiatrist) will prevail. However, there is a very meaningful way in which the human rights tradition may promote the structural/cultural approach: in ensuring that those who want to build alternative structures and live according to other cultures will not be too greatly impeded from doing so. More concretely, one might pick up the argument made in sections 3 and 7 of chapter 3 about a human right to "alternative ways of life" experiments, generally on the increase in the Western world precisely because of the threat to human integrity stemming from the dominant, "bourgeois way of life." Much more concretely, this would imply such instruments as:

1   some minimum assistance in acquiring land and houses, e.g. for commune-type living;
2   ensuring that it is not illegal or difficult from any point of view to re-establish non-monetary economies, e.g. by growing food oneself, exchanging goods and services on a non-market basis, etc.;
3   not interfering unduly with social demands on people who prefer in this way to lead a life less threatening to mental and somatic health.

Such matters may, eventually, be pointers to the future, including a future with less mental disorder. A state could, for instance, provide health through exercise and healing diet, by building thousands of kilometers of hiking and bicycling trails and subsidizing organically grown food. The *how* does matter.

On the International Structure of Torture

What follow are some notes by somebody more knowledgeable about international structure than about torture, possibly useful for those whose knowledge has the opposite profile.[4] The notes were written in 1974. Since then the world structure has changed, possibly for the better. The analysis of the world of 1974 has been retained; the basic approach being structural, not tied to particular country actors.

At that time the basic structure of the world took the form of two relatively parallel vertical blocs. There was capitalist imperialism, with the US, Japan and the EC countries in the center (and the US in the center of the center, so to speak), and most of the Third World countries in the periphery. Then there were some countries with a relatively recent successful history of liberation (China 1949, Cuba 1959, to a large extent Algeria 1962, and some others), and other countries that tried in vain (Iran 1951–3, Guatemala 1954, Dominican Republic 1965, Chile 1969). And there was social imperialism, with the Soviet Union in the center and most of Eastern Europe, Mongolia, and (partly) Cuba in the periphery. They also had countries with a relatively recent successful history of liberation (China 1958–60, once again, the only country to have achieved it twice without the aid of a world war, Yugoslavia in 1948, Albania 1960) and other countries that tried in vain (Hungary 1956, Czechoslovakia 1968).

The assumption is that these structures were tremendously important to the ruling elites in the center countries, and that they would do almost everything to maintain them. For this purpose they have their bridgeheads in the periphery, predominantly political and economic elites under capitalist imperialism, and predominantly political and military elites under social imperialism – but with all three elites coming into full play in both cases under crises.

The classical way of controlling the periphery is well known: gunboat diplomacy, military intervention (send in the marines, Tank-Kommunismus – as opposed to Gulasch-Kommunismus) from the center to the periphery, with the Dominican Republic in 1965 and Czechoslovakia in 1968 being disturbingly similar. But these methods came increasingly into disrepute, for many reasons. They exposed the center states too much. The EU member countries, thus, had practically speaking abandoned them (with the important exception of the residual colonialism of France in Chad and some other places), and Portugal could join the EU only after such methods had come to an end (it finally became a member, with Spain, in 1986). Moreover, the methods were dangerous: they could lead to confrontation between the two centers (so-called East–West superpower conflict). The center populations might also oppose governmental interventionist policies, particularly if they did not win quickly (the Indochina wars fought by France and the US, France in Algeria, and later, the Soviet Union in Afghanistan).

The obvious next tactic would be to train the local bridgeheads and tie them so closely to the center through all kinds of benefits (and costs if they do not succeed) that they will carry out the counter-insurgency job, in their own interest and that of the center. This they will do partly in their own country, as in the case of Brazil in 1964, partly also in other countries as in the case of Iran (the Dhofar "rebellion"). The tremendous input in equipment and training of the Latin American military had this as its major (or only) function, and similar things were taking place in Africa, particularly in the former French colonies. When chains of repression across borders are created this way, one can talk about sub-imperialism (the Iranian case). What shows up is often, wrongly, referred to as "local wars."

The use of torture and its tremendous increase recently should be seen in this perspective. The term "torture" is used relatively broadly. It takes place at the micro level, a cell in a basement, the torturer against the tortured, with only a few people in either role. Like punishment, torture is intended to control the victims (individual prevention) and other people's behavior (general prevention) so that they do not try to upset the structure mentioned, nationally *and* internationally. The most common forms of torture inflict tremendous pain, and there is the additional purpose of extracting information about activities directed against the status quo. But other forms of torture, e.g. trying to prove to the person that what he or she fights for is a lost cause, hopeless, meaningless, do not inflict physical pain; and the purpose is not necessarily to extract information, but for instance to break his or her will. More recent psychological techniques should be included in the concept of torture since they seem to be on the increase.

The first thesis would be that torture as a method of control through killing and repression will tend to flow along the well-known lines of imperialistic dominance. This means:

1 *torture hardware* would flow along trade lines, within some type of multinational corporation, from production sites in the center to the periphery; well camouflaged, like the production of napalm;
2 *torture software*, the training of personnel, would take place within the framework of existing training programs within the two vertical blocs mentioned, i.e. military assistance programs and police training programs;
3 *torture research* to assess the efficacy of torture, meaningless without the participation of specialists in biology and the medical and behavioral sciences, would be transmitted within the chan-

nels of scientific communication, not in public international conferences, but by using the ties established through fellowship programs, participation in joint research ventures, etc.

The second thesis would be that the use of macro-control (regular warfare) might complement that of micro-control (counter-insurgency, including the use of torture) for the purposes of maintaining these vertical blocs. Macro-control becomes increasingly inapplicable against people's and national wars of liberation. War is designed for other types of conflict, viz. between states roughly equal in power and technological capacity. On the other hand, in the vertical settings of the two types of imperialism, micro-control is applicable, increasingly sophisticated and research- and capital-intensive, but not yet so much so that it can be practiced locally without a permanent flow of hardware, software, and research from the center. In short, it is compatible with a low profile, provided the bridgeheads are reliable and efficient.

It cannot be assumed that all bridgeheads are equally reliable and efficient. Hence, the third thesis is that there will be regional bridgeheads in the field of torture, as in the fields of economic, military, and political transactions. Micro-control could be obtained in Chile (1973) by means of torturers and interrogators from Brazil, but trained partly by the US; on the Arab side of the Persian Gulf by means of Savak torturers and interrogators from Iran also benefiting from US training, etc.; in Cuba (in the early 1960s) by the feared G2, trained by Czech specialists who in turn had received training in Moscow, and so on. The pattern of two-step sub-imperialism would show up in torture as in other chains of control, the obvious hypothesis being (in 1974) that Brazil and Iran are regional bridgeheads for Latin America and the Middle East respectively. For the Soviet Union one would assume direct bilateral lines of control, in line with the general Soviet policy of avoiding a regional center in Eastern Europe. Indirect control is neither necessary, because of the low number of countries involved and the short distances, nor desirable because such a regional center might also serve Eastern European separatism. It should be noted that Portuguese Brazil can never play that role for Spanish South America as a whole, nor can Persian Iran for all Arab Muslim countries.

Thus, it is generally to be expected, and that is the fourth thesis, that torture may continue to be on the increase precisely because of the change in repression strategy. Generally, with each arms control agreement an increase is to be expected in the means of micro-control – not only torture, but also such counter-insurgency techniques as seismic footstep detectors, body-sniffers, electronic battle-fields, etc. ("low intensity conflict"). Hence, torture has increasingly to be discussed in its international structural context, not merely as a problem of infraction of human rights in the country where torture shows up, but as one of the strategies of capitalist and social imperialism.

It follows from this that not much is to be expected when it comes to putting an end to torture before these structures have been removed. Given imperialist repression, the alternative to torture would be some other means of repression, e.g. collective mind control. It also follows that appeals to human values and declarations are likely to remain as ineffective as traditional pacifist appeals have been in connection with the arms race. Arms are produced partly because those who order them think there will be a use for them, and partly because it pays to produce them. In the same vein, torture evolves because those in whose interest it is to repress continue to see it as a means of maintaining the status quo, used by the designers of training programs for military and police agencies, and studied by scientists fascinated with human behavior under extreme conditions (like the Auschwitz physicians and their Japanese counterparts).

Finally, it follows from this that to obtain more information about torture and how to fight it (short of destroying imperialist structures), one should get more insight into what happens above the level of the torture chamber, not neglecting the testimony of the tortured and the confessions of the torturers. More particularly, there should be an intensive search for people willing to reveal the secrets of:

1 the production system for torture hardware – people working in the factories and shipping the products;
2 the training system for torture software – people participating as teachers or students in national and international systems of this type of military and police training;
3 the research system, with special focus on teams where center and periphery scientists cooperate across disciplinary borders, e.g. electronics specialists with social scientists.

A system of international awards should be established, even giving monetary rewards to those who are willing to volunteer such information, especially against their own governments. A system of political resistance (including asylum, and a promise not to prosecute for prior participation in the research, development, production and practice of torture) to those who refuse to continue to participate, and even denounce publicly what they have been participating in, might also be made available.

Conclusion

There is a structure to torture, not only nationally but also internationally. A relevant human rights tradition certainly has to condemn torture and protect the victim. But it also has to condemn the structures producing the torture, and protect those who try to reveal and demolish those structures. The right not to be tortured is basic, but also shallow. The deeper right would be the human right to live in a social and world structure that does not produce torture. Obviously, the two do not exclude each other.

As a matter of fact, and as pointed out in the preceding chapter, the admirable (and largely unused) formulation in article 28 of the Universal Declaration of Human Rights ("Everyone is entitled to a social and international order in which the rights and freedoms set forth in this Declaration can be fully realized") points in the right direction (in conjuntion with article 5: "No one shall be subjected to torture or to cruel, inhuman or degrading treatment or punishment.").

HUMAN RIGHTS AND THE STRUCTURE OF ECOLOGICAL BALANCE

How simple it would be if we could address the problem of ecological degradation in terms of polluters and depleters, establish universal norms of upper limits for pollution and depletion consonant with the concept of "sustainable development," organize a world detection system for infraction of these norms, arraign those who infract them in a world court (which could ultimately be the International Court of Justice), and then let the polluters (and depleters) pay, or even suffer imprisonment. Social evils would be conceived of in terms of evil acts, and behind evil acts the evil actors would be identified and punished, to change their evil ways or at least to frighten others with similar evil intentions. And as a result we could hand over to our children, or at least our grandchildren, the badly needed clean environment to which they would be entitled.

No doubt this paradigm captures something: the tip of the iceberg not only in the sense of being visible, but also in the sense that the most visible actors may also be the worst. But a structure consists of myriads of actions, including non-actions and acts of omission. They all somehow add up, or multiply, to the well-known problems of ecological deterioration today: decrease in bio-diversity, genetic erosion, ozone layer thinning,[5] deforestation/desertification syndromes, global warming,[6] toxic pollution, human overpopulation.[7] By the logic of the actor-orientated paradigm the evil actor and the evil act are the cause. But an assumed cause should be proportionate to the magnitude of such consequences. No single act has such a grotesque consequence: the threat to all life on earth. Punishment, even the removal of some polluters and depleters from the economic cycles, seems inadequate to the task of protecting the needs of life in general and human life in particular.

To probe more deeply into the problem, consider table 4.4's method of classifying current symptoms of general eco-deterioration. The list is the same as that in the preceding paragraph,

Table 4.4 Some current symptoms of eco-deterioration

	Decreasing diversity	Decreasing symbiosis
Increasing depletion	Bio-diversity decrease Genetic erosion	Ozone layer thinning Deforestation/ desertification
Increasing pollution	Global warming Toxic pollution	Human overpopulation Toxic pollution

save that "toxic pollution" (and not only to human beings, but to all forms of life) appears twice. But another deeper perspective has been added to depletion/pollution: decreasing diversity and decreasing symbiosis. The thinning of the ozone layer, deforestation and some of the toxic pollution threatening the symbiotic basis for life on earth: photosynthesis. In addition, human beings do not at present live symbiotically with the rest of nature, and ever more human beings ever less so. At the same time the diversity is decreased through erosion, flooding, and pollution. However we analyze the causes of eco-deterioration the effects hit deeply, thus underlining the urgency of the matter.

But that in itself is no reason to add a structure-orientated perspective. Murderers also hit deeply in the psycho-structure of the bereaved; they can still be understood and to some extent handled adequately within an actor-orientated paradigm. The cause and effect of murder are of the same order of magnitude, even if we continue the search for deeper causes.

We obtain another perspective on eco-deterioration by asking why that problem is so important today. Tentative answer: because (global) *industrialism* has brought in its wake industrial and household waste high on anorganic and synthetic organic matter that is not biodegradable, and because (global) *commercialism* has brought in its wake economic cycles so world-encompassing and opaque that nobody really knows where a problem starts and where it ends. There are causes and effects all over the place and formulas such as "the causes are local, the effects are global" are misleading. The causes may be in a demand–supply nexus connecting people in all parts of the world, and they may cause deterioration at some very local place somewhere. Or both cause and effect may be global. Or both local.

The process perspective, over time, would lead us to ask whether, if the root cause is ever-expanding global industrialism and commercialism, and the culture underlying this, the remedy might be a return to more organically based, local eco-cycles where enzymes can still handle production and consumption waste, and the distance from cause to effect is so short that people become aware of the negative consequences of actions located in their own neighborhood and easily identify the source of the problem.

To the objection that only very few want to return to pre-industrial revolution days, however idyllic that rural life is portrayed as being, one answer might be to make waste biodegradable through new methods (including new enzymes and bacteria; but then, are *they* biodegradable?), and by switching to renewable resources. With such measures enacted all over, much industrialism and commercialism can survive. But the focus here is not on solving these problems but on how to think about them and act upon them, and the possible role of the human rights tradition in masking or solving the problem.

If increasing industrialism and commercialism are the underlying causes, four points follow immediately:

1 *Adequacy.* With this type of explanation a cause has been identified of the same magnitude as the effects so that the proportionality criterion is satisfied.
2 *Structure.* These are structures and, like all structures, in process. With many billions of people involved, and myriads of acts, industrialists and merchants are fully entitled to claim innocence on the basis that their actions are parts of larger structures and that the products they offer, with pollution and depletion as side-effects, are heavily demanded.
3 *Rootedness.* These structures are at the very heart of the social formation referring to itself as "modern," or even "post-modern," far from being a tail or an appendix that can be easily removed, leaving the body intact, even more healthy. Any fundamental change of that structure is tantamount to changing the social formation. Consequently, the likely approach is tampering with, rather than transforming, the structure.
4 *Ambiguity.* These are some of the structures that constitute the basis for the high level of material living in the more developed countries. Their yin/yang nature, good *and* bad, should surprise nobody except epistemological hardliners who believe the world comes nicely sorted in good *or* bad. Only transformation, not removal, can be on the political agenda.

Fears that these four points will cut deep are not unfounded. The actor-orientated perspective offers a rationale for how to tamper rather than how to transform, one reason for acceptance of that perspective. But tampering will not deliver the goods: a clean, sustainable environment.

If human beings are supposed to have a *right* to a clean environment, that right should imply a claim on the actors behind acts of commission, *in casu* acts of pollution and depletion, or, more correctly, on the authorities that have received (meaning accepted) this norm and are obliged to see to it that the right is fulfilled. But there should also be a claim on those who through their acts of omission fail to do what is necessary to avoid at least the worst eco-catastrophes.

A structure serves as a consciousness-reducing device: people do things because "everybody does them," and they themselves "have always done it." In other words, we are dealing with behavior rather than with action, or, more precisely, with half-acts shading into reflexive behavior that comes about as a response when the structural stimuli are present. Through consciousness-formation the process may be reversed, the behavior becoming fully conscious action. What happens today in the field of the environment is precisely that kind of consciousness-formation. To smoke in public, even in crowded places, may have been behavior yesterday, but today it is action, even an act of commission. To fail to move to a private area where smoking may be permitted is an act of omission, but still an act. To fail to do what can be done to transform structures that produce eco-deterioration or stand in the way, as obstacles, to efforts to improve the situation, would also be an act of omission. There are myriads of them. The human right to a clean environment demands that the correct actions are undertaken. Not to do so is complicity with the wrongdoing, even if engaged in by many.

HUMAN RIGHTS AND THE STRUCTURE OF PEACE

Let us now try to apply this kind of reasoning to the problems of peace and war. Again the same situation: how simple it would be if all that was needed was to couch the problem in terms of aggressors and victims, establish norms for aggression, organize a world detection and adjudication machinery (again, the latter could be the International Court of Justice rather than the Security Council, in order to use legal rather than political criteria), and punish aggressors, partly to incapacitate them, partly to "teach them a lesson," and partly to teach others a lesson. Again, much is captured in this paradigm, but not all. What is missing?

If we make a comparison with the preceding section about ecological balance we see immediately that there is less of a problem of disproportion between cause and effect. One single war may be said to be a phenomenon of the same order of magnitude as the country actors, usually governments, at the beginning of the causal chain. But the institution of war, throughout the centuries, even millennia, is of a higher order of magnitude, transcending any particular aggressor–victim system. There are deeper causes at work.

Nevertheless, it makes more sense to hold a country responsible for an attack on another than to hold some economic actors in manufacture and/or trade responsible for the calamities listed today as eco-catastrophes. In clear-cut cases economic actor A may be held responsible for some specific eco-deterioration. But such clear-cut cases are becoming increasingly rare: there are too complex cycles in space, too much accumulation over time. The economic actor can hide behind the structure.

Can the aggressor also hide behind a structure? There certainly is structural violence in the sense that unintended damage is done to individuals and countries, all over the world, at all times; the 40,000 children dying every day from avoidable causes (malnutrition, lack of hygiene) are a clear example. That violence should certainly be reduced, and that reduction of violence has been more or less identified with development in the first section of this chapter. As with ecology the point has been made that except in some clear-cut cases it may not make much sense to hold concrete actors responsible. Some perpetrators can use this, saying: what I do is nothing compared with what is going on every hour, every day, 365 days a year . . .

But the nagging question is not the relative size of the individual act and the total problem. The murderer can also claim that his or her act is nothing compared to what else is going on. The problem is whether the aggressor is embedded in structures, with cultures leaving him or her no choice. And murderers, except at war as soldiers or when hired, cannot claim innocence as part of structures demanding their "services," as can the polluters.

Of course aggression, like anything else, is caused, and of course some of those causes are structural, some cultural. Colonialism is such a structure, linking colony and colonial power. The former may revolt to become free, the latter may repress, before (pre-emption) or after the revolt (reaction). Do those causes justify the aggression, however, and, if not, did the aggressor have a choice; could he or she will non-aggression, or was will-power suspended by the causes? In short, were there mitigating circumstances?

These two considerations do not exclude each other. All four combinations are well known in the legal tradition:

1 aggression unjustified, there was a choice: the clear case for applying the classical legal paradigm;

2 aggression unjustified, there was no choice: the case of the
   permanent aggressor (for whatever reason – physiological, psychological, socio-cultural), the bully;
3 aggression justified, there was a choice: the argument could still
   be made that the aggression should have been expressed non-
   violently;
4 aggression justified, there was no choice: the case could be made
   for reduced or no punishment (a crime of passion, for example?).

The problem is to what extent a parallel can be drawn between
municipal and international law at this crucial point; all the time
keeping in mind that the goal is a world where the right to live in
peace is implemented. People should have reasons to feel safe. The
legal paradigm applies to case 1 above. But what kind of paradigms
do we need for the other three cases?

This is not the place to enter into the complexity of violence and
peace theory. But let us look at three theories, one diachronic, two
more synchronic.[8] Thus, there is the old set of propositions to the
effect that *violence breeds violence*. Collectivities, e.g. nations, have
a very long memory. An act of violence committed against them can
lead to revenge generations later; the former Yugoslavia in the early
1990s being a horrifying example. Collectivities such as families and
clans also have long memories; at that level the same phenomenon is
known as vendetta. The chains of violence against the "arch-enemy"
may spin through centuries.

A third party trying to break a cycle of violence by establishing a
cut-off point, naming the aggressor at that point in time as *the*
aggressor, will be seen as intervening on behalf of the other side and
become a party to the deadly game. Conclusion: a warning against
naming one actor as the aggressor, focusing attention on the process
within which the violence unfolds.

The threat of violence, or the perceived threat of violence, may
reinforce the cycle of violence (almost) as much as violence itself.
One mechanism would be based on the ideology that to deter
violence counter-violence has to be prepared; *si vis pacem, para
bellum*. But preparation may lead to counter-preparations if the
intentions are perceived as aggressive rather than defensive. The
spiral of mutual provocation through preparation may then unleash
violence. One possible conclusion: *si vis pacem, para pacem*.

Another approach would take as the point of departure the extent
to which direct violence is rooted in structure and culture, and then

remove the factors that seem to be conducive to violence. A conflict may be rooted in the structure, as between buyers and sellers of labor, or of raw materials, over the terms of exchange. Or a conflict can be seen as rooted in the state system itself, with its monopoly of violence vested in states that easily set a collision course over interests and values. If the conflicts are not solved creatively, and the (political) culture defines violence as legitimate in such situations, then structure implies conflict implies violence. But conflicts do not necessarily lead to violence; that depends more on the culture.

Conclusion

The road to peace goes through creative conflict resolution, which usually means transformation of some structures, and through the substitution of peace cultures for violence cultures, delegitimizing violence. The use of violence to punish the aggressor neither solves conflicts nor delegitimizes violence. On the contrary, it probably freezes the conflict and legitimizes violence. In other words, it is not only *not* productive of human rights implementation but even counterproductive, as though the fines imposed on polluters were themselves polluting (and the argument may be that indirectly they are: by pushing the costs on to the customers small consumers may be eliminated, making room for bigger consumers with more consumer waste).

The right to live in peace can be read as the right not to be a victim of aggression. But if we assume that aggression is not random but caused by structural and cultural factors between and within the actors, then the right to live in peace is the right to live in a social setting (in the words of article 28 of the Universal Declaration of Human Rights, "a social and international order") where something is done about factors, not only actors. The difficulty of the legal tradition in handling them is not solved by arguing that structural and cultural changes are political rather than legal problems. The truth is, both are both. Segregation in the Southern United States and apartheid in South Africa were structures upheld by cultures of arrogance; impeding human rights implementation. People were entitled to the removal of these obstacles. In the end not to remove them, an act of omission, became illegal. Hopefully, peace problems will also eventually graduate from actor-orientated only to include structure/culture-orientated approaches.

POINTERS TO THE FUTURE: THE INSTITUTION/ STRUCTURE DIALECTIC

Actor-orientated thinking leads to institutions to handle evil actors, structure/culture-orientated thinking to politics to change wrong structures and aggressive cultures; is that all there is to it? No, what has been indicated in the last two sections is that the situation is not so dichotomous as one might have been led to believe, including from the way this subject was introduced in the first and second sections of chapter 2. Structures (collective patterns of action and interaction) and cultures (collective codes we live by and act according to) are not immutable. They are changing, otherwise human history would be biology with action and interaction derived from bio-genetic codes only, immutable except for genetic mutations. Moreover, both structure and culture may be deliberately changed. Media culture in general, and TV culture in particular, do not have to be that violent; they can be changed, and probably will be when ultimately the findings relating media violence to real-life violence penetrate. And the media do not have to portray reality with such an actor-orientated bias; they have a choice and may find a better balance when insights into structures and how they work on us penetrate.

As it is today, structures – "everybody does it"/"we always did it" – look iron-clad and persons look small, like the traditional Chinese paintings with overpowering nature and very tiny humans. We know that if enough people turn against them in violent or (preferably) non-violent revolutions they may be overturned, as were slavery and colonialism. But how can we understand them from the angle of the legal tradition?

We should perhaps, first point out that the legal tradition is itself enacted within a structure, and upheld by a culture. In that structure actors are defined generically, not by proper names but by their status: "defendant," "attorney at law," "prosecutor," "judge," etc. This definition *in abstracto* is essential for the whole distinction between "the rule of men" and "the rule of law."[9] A legal tradition with predictability (which is a condition for being exactly that, a "tradition") has to transcend the individual, historical persons in any concrete case, criminal or civil. As for all other social institutions the structure solves that problem, embedded in a culture filled with prescriptions and proscriptions about how to act so as to fulfill the requirements of "due process."

The problem is that the cases handled by the legal tradition are seen as exactly that, cases. They exhibit patterns in the sense of being similar, permitting classifications which trigger juridical precedents covered in the sources of law. But the basic unit of discourse is a juridical person and the problem to be decided is whether the juridical persons have acted correctly relative to the legal norms governing their action.

However, the legal tradition also produces legal norms; meaning defining structures designed to transcend any given case, being compatible with similar structures in the past and a possible model for structures in the future. Moreover, there are meta-norms defining what constitute right and wrong structures based on legal norms. In short, within the tradition structure and culture are by no means unknown. And yet the approach is not good at handling structures outside the legal institution.

Four approaches emerge from the exploration thus far:

1   *The worst actor approach* – the tip of the iceberg visible even with unguided, actor-orientated eyes. However, instead of only arguing the exceptionalism of the case, how bad that actor is, the case should be used also to point to the structural/cultural aspects. Slave-owners who beat their slaves extraordinarily are often evil as individuals, and at the same time structurally slave-owners and culturally products of their time; but for structure and culture they might never have had slaves to beat; be that rarely, often, or extraordinarily often. There is still a case for a verdict of guilty and a sentence. The structural/cultural point has to be argued in such a way as to allow for a discussion of the general case – the bad, the worse, and the worst – without justifying the defendant who evidently had a choice and who otherwise would not have been among the worst.

2   *Arraign the structure in court* – meaning that the unit that appears in court is, at the very least, a dyad, two actors. The defendant, if that is the word, would be the relationship between them. If we call the parties topdog/underdog, or *Herr/Knecht*, then the simplest case would be the topdog/*Herr* producing the arguments in favor of and the underdog/*Knecht* the arguments against the

existing relation. Reality may be more complex, with both arguing for and against, or changing roles, perhaps indicating that the relationship was not as simple as some might have assumed. If found guilty, the judge could still deliver actor-orientated sentences: "anyone who enacts this kind of structure will be sentenced to . . ." A more appropriate conclusion might aim at structural transformation. This approach may then be fed into the third approach, below. In the same vein a culture could be arraigned in court, feeding into the fourth approach, below.

3 *The structural approach* – which would consist of showing what the structure is like, how it works automatically to deprive large numbers of people of their human rights day in and day out, and how an alternative structure would produce better results from human rights points of view; a double-pronged critical/ constructive approach. Empirical evidence for the latter would be useful but plausibility would be based on empirical evidence for the former, the critique. An example is the US Supreme Court's desegregation decision of 17 May 1954. Constructive use of article 28 of the Universal Declaration of Human Rights ("social and international order") with deep and broad implications may serve as a base.

4 *The cultural approach* – which would do exactly the same for culture. Sooner or later it is bound to arise in relation to TV violence in particular; the question is only where and when.

When it is shown to the satisfaction of competent men and women that certain structures and cultures are as argued, the next step would be to identify who are delaying the change by acts of commission, sufficient to maintain the wrong structures, and who in positions of responsibility are, by acts of omission, failing to do what is necessary to change them. An educated guess would be, of course, that both categories are among those who benefit from the structure materially or non-materially. But that should be only a first hypothesis, overlooking, as it does, enlightened elements among those who subjectively are oppressors depriving others of human rights, and accomplices in the oppression among the oppressed. Moreover, the point is less to arraign the actors in court than to give them a warning and a period of grace to put their structure/culture in order, through processes of transformation. Those processes are political in nature since politics is about power, and structures, too, are power arrangements.

In any single, concrete case there may then be room for a discussion of the relative causal weight of the three factors: the actors as such, the structure, and the culture. All kinds of conclusions are possible, from the three pure models via mixes of two to the combination of all three. Perpetrators may learn to hide behind structures and cultures. But if they do the chances that structures and cultures are arraigned in court with them, as indicated here, should increase, and more so the more open the protest against the human rights deprivation. In other words, the small (actor) fish may escape scot-free, but in so doing clear the ground for catching the big (structure and culture) fish. Evidently those protecting the latter may prefer to sacrifice an actor once in a while, even a big one, hoping to deflect the attention of the courts and the public at large.

Today anything but the first of the four approaches mentioned above sounds rather unrealistic. But most human-made things around us were unrealistic at one time, often only a short while ago. A dialectic like that indicated above is almost bound to come, even if, as argued on page 50 above, both (deep) structures and (deep) cultures are extremely intractable.

Here is a scenario. Certain human rights violations are traced back to those intractable aspects of the human condition:[10] structure and culture. The instrument for doing so might be a commission, national and international, publicly appointed, drawing on experts, and politicians and others representing "common sense." Legally trained professionals should definitely be on it. A next step would be the public hearing. Usually such hearings are held by the legislative branch of government, possibly by the relevant part of the executive. Why not by the judiciary? There would be at least two good reasons: judges are good at weighing evidence, and the kind of arguments that arise might play a considerable role in later court cases. Again the example would be the US Supreme Court decision of 17 May 1954, establishing a case against a structure: that of segregated schooling.

The next step would be to return to concrete cases and the actor-orientated perspective. The structure, not being a juridical person, cannot be found guilty, only wrong. But those who uphold the structure through their action or fail to dismantle it through their inaction can be found guilty.

In short, the structure/institution dialectic starts with a structure (or a culture) that escapes the institution, and with culprits hiding behind it. Other institutions, but also the legal institutions, adopt a structure-orientated mode and attack the structure, using worst cases and normal cases. They then switch back to the actor-orientated mode, with a new basis for conventional legal action. And await the next turn of the dialectic.

5

HUMAN RIGHTS AND SOCIAL PROCESSES

THE STATE SYSTEM, THE CORPORATE SYSTEM, AND CIVIL SOCIETY

Modern society has three major components, state, capital, and people, and the last can be seen as organized in all kinds of associations that add up to civil society. All three are evolving, never stable in spite of control efforts. Thus, socialism in Eastern Europe and the former Soviet Union was an effort to legitimize only one part of civil society, the Communist Party, put it in charge of the state and the rest of civil society, and put the state in charge of capital. The formation was in static but unstable equilibrium. When it collapsed it disintegrated completely, and civil society and capital started sprouting, particularly the former, having been repressed so long.

At the international level the three are reproduced as intergovernmental organizations (IGOs), in a hierarchy with the UN at the top; as transnational corporations (TNCs), in an informal hierarchy according to assets;[1] and as international non-governmental, or people's organizations (INGOs, IPOs), in an informal hierarchy according to size of membership,[2] like states.[3]

Combining the two levels we get the state system (with the IGOs), the corporate system (with the TNCs) and the civil society system (with the INGOs or IPOs). Some kind of global governance[4] is slowly emerging from the former, and a world civil society[5] from the latter, and something may also take shape for the corporate world. But the process toward global governance is clearly biased in favor of the state system, using the world civil society in a consultative/advisory capacity, and by and large having the corporate system operate from the sidelines, as lobbies, financing the actors they prefer, etc.

The problem is how these three components of modern society, today found in one form or the other all over the world, handle the human rights discourse. The general bias, as elaborated in chapter 1, is very much in favor of the state system and the top-heavy "alpha channel." Let us now add to that analysis.

In principle all three can be perpetrators, all three can be victims, and all three can help to reinforce human rights. But since these are human rights, of people and peoples, we would generally assume the victims to be people, and people *live* in civil society. They would be the party most interested in reinforcing the rights. Consequently, state and capital will easily be cast in the roles as perpetrators. But the state has by the very nature of the human rights construction the role of reinforcing the norms; being held accountable to the norm-producer, the UN, with its subdivisions for human rights.

Table 5.1　The three actors and the three human rights roles

Actor	State	Capital	Civil society
Perpetrator	Yes	Yes	No
Victim	No	Yes	Yes
Reinforcer	Yes	No	Yes

Schematically we arrive at something similar to table 5.1. Needless to say, the state can certainly also be a victim, of external aggression and of internal warfare. But the former is presumably the province of international law, and the latter is usually seen as "politics," meaning governed by other types of rules. And people, in civil society, can be perpetrators, but that is handled under criminal law unless directed against the state, in which case we are again talking about "politics." The three profiles are very different, a diversity in principle to be celebrated, illustrating the problems and potentials of a complex world construction where the state system is but a part.

Thus, as already pointed out: the state, highly visible on the stage of the human rights drama, is cast in the ambiguous role in relation to human rights of sometimes violating the norms it is supposed to reinforce.[6] From inside the country this may lead to civil unrest, with civil society trying to reinforce.[7] However, if the state really has the monopoly on means of violence this may not be easy, leading to the use of outside state system mechanisms: resolutions spelling out the normative expectations from the norm-producer, the UN (and the Human Rights Commission); economic sanctions and/or military intervention in the name of human rights.[8]

And this is where capital enters the stage. Economic sanctions imply the negative use of capital: no investment, no trade, no financial transactions. Capital is not reinforcing; its absence is made use of to reinforce, and may be added to the list of victims, one possible reason that they may want to compensate by making profits from military intervention, as suppliers of all kinds of services, including transport and the arms themselves.

This raises the general question whether capital has not been underutilized as an instrument for reinforcing human rights. Capital could be very effective in containing a delinquent state, by withholding corporate taxes, and goods and services in general. After all, one of its old roles was as supplier to the state and the predecessors of the state: the king or emperor.[9] There may well be situations when the state can do without popular consent, but not without the corporations in general and the banks in particular.

Civil society also enters in a double role: as victim, and as reinforcer. In an excellent survey article by Chad Alger[10] the now classical anti-slavery and anti-colonialism campaigns, both of them successful, are seen as among the first in this tradition. Whereas the state may be paralyzed by the conflict of interest between the temptation to break human rights and the obligation to reinforce them, civil society experiences no such conflict of interest. To be a victim of human rights violations and to want human rights implemented are highly compatible. From this alone follow civil society enthusiasm and state system ambivalence. And the conclusion is obvious: without the civil society, the NGOs, human rights as an institution would be vacuous in many countries, perhaps most, perhaps all.

But that thesis can also be read backwards as demonstrated by the ex-socialist and many Third World countries today. The human rights gave civil society more substance, as human rights watchers, even watchdogs, like fox-terriers watching their masters keenly, barking and biting the kicking legs when needed, sometimes at considerable risk to themselves. But are they equipped to do this? And do they have a mandate?

The second question leads to a double paradox: if they had a mandate they might also be seated in the major articulation of civil society in the state, the national assembly. But if there are elections with secret ballot there is probably also less of a human rights problem, at least for the civil-political rights. On the other hand, the national assembly may fail as a watchdog being very close to the other two parts of the state construction, sometimes a kicking leg rather than a fox-terrier. The human rights organizations are needed everywhere; this dialectic never ends.

In the Western countries human rights have generally first been articulated by civil society, and the state has received the norms only when they can be seen as being sent from above, and usually without any enthusiasm.[11] The civil-political rights were promoted by powerful individuals and civil groups from the emerging bourgeoisie who then became majorities in the national assemblies, transforming monarchies into presidential systems or constitutional monarchies. The economic-social-cultural rights were promoted by working-class parties before the ruling classes could accept them from a national assembly. In the same vein the most articulate and meaningful civil society organizations today are probably in the fields of development, environment, and peace, promoting norms about goals and processes that sooner or later will be accepted by the state system. The peace organizations have a very difficult task here since the norms they promulgate also regulate the way states behave relative to other states and through that to their own citizens.[12] But one day they will prevail.

Are the people's organizations equipped to carry out these important functions? Again the same paradox: if they were very well equipped there would probably have been less of a problem. As long as they are against the flow rather than mainstream they have to exude normative power, not the power of the stick or the carrot; that is for state and capital to exercise. Funding from their own government easily makes them governmental non-governmental organizations, GNGOs, steeped in ambiguity. Funding from other states, from the ubiquitous Nordic countries for example, is some kind of interference in internal affairs; not unproblematic. Funding from the UN, the norm-sender *par excellence*, would seem more logical. Funding from all three, and even more sources, may be the best solution.

BLUE, RED, AND GREEN GENERATION RIGHTS – AND THEN WHAT?

The civil-political rights (10 December 1948 – the Universal Declaration) and the economic-social-cultural rights (16 December 1966 – the ESC Covenant) are often referred to as the first- and the second-generation rights, with the solidarity rights (to development, clean environment and peace) as a possible third generation. The distinction makes sense if "generation" is given a historical-political agenda interpretation, implying new issues rather than new approaches.

For one perspective on "generation" consider the following image of the feudal/early modern European social formation (and beyond).

1 Clergy – side-tracked by secularization.
2 Aristocracy – *the zero generation*: challenged the Church.
3 Bourgeoisie – *first generation*: challenged the aristocracy.
4 Peasants, workers – *second generation*: challenged the bourgeoisie.
5 Women and children, other peoples, nature – *third generation*: challenged the technocracy.
6 Non-West – *fourth generation*: challenging the West.

The European social formation is here seen as a layer-cake. The first, second and third estates are on top, but the third is split into bourgeoisie proper (the people living inside the *Burg*, the walled city, such as merchants and artisans), peasants and workers, then women and children, then other peoples[13] and nature (which may be split into animals and plants, minerals, water, and air and space), and finally the Non-West, with similar divisions.

History, process, enters the picture with each layer challenging the layer above, transforming the cake although it remains a layer-cake.[14] Each process defines a political generation, starting with a "zero" generation, aristocracy which put the Church on a side-track through a process that took centuries (from the thirteenth to the seventeenth in Britain), paving the way for secular power.

If we now see expressions of the first generation in the US and French constitutions of 1776–87 and 1789 respectively, then we are dealing with two different ways of establishing a liberal-capitalist social formation: by escaping (by ship) from conservative-feudal society (US) or by destroying it (France). In either case the bourgeoisie rises, liberated from the second and first layers. In what was to become the US the recruitment was from layer 4, working classes, building layer 3, leaving the aristocracy in England somewhat lonely, increasingly marginalized and impoverished. The French aristocracy joined the bourgeoisie and became managers in state and capital.

The Universal Declaration of 10 December 1948 is a reaffirmation of these values, threatened not only by the Axis powers that had been defeated three years earlier, but also by the specter of communism. Property rights are enshrined in article 17(1) – "Everyone has the right to own property alone as well as in association with others" – and (2): "No one shall be arbitrarily deprived of his property." The formulation is in exact parallel with article 15 about "the right to a nationality" of which "no one shall be arbitrarily deprived" either.[15]

Up came the bourgeoisie, the carrier of the capitalist system, protected by a liberal logic where "everyone is entitled to all the rights and freedoms set forth in this Declaration, without distinction of any kind, such as . . . *property, birth or other status*" (article 2, emphasis added).[16] But they had not liberated themselves from "birth or other status" to be enslaved by an overpowering state, so they set out immediately also to limit the powers of the state. What they forgot, naturally, was that capitalism could enslave others, including the capitalists themselves.

So the red came up challenging the blue, as mentioned. Trade unions and the working classes, peasants and workers challenged the bourgeoisie, and liberalism was challenged by social democrat, socialist, and communist ideologies, and also by the remnants of pre-1789 feudal conservatism. The second generation of human rights has much of the signature of the working class and other under-privileged groups (non-whites, women, children, indigenous peoples) that became a part of liberal-bourgeois-capitalist society, but also of the liberal ability to integrate challenges, which is exactly that, liberal. But the second generation of rights is not that different from the first, reflecting how the working class was absorbed by the bourgeoisie and, ultimately, after 1989, the socialist countries by the capitalist countries.[17]

Precisely for that reason a new class emerges with a new agenda, those alienated by the historical compromise between the blue and the red in its social (state cooperating with capital, capital with workers) and ideological manifestations (the social democrat/technocrat compromise). Typically, they would be people concerned with how a capitalist society that had come to terms with its own working classes nevertheless posed threats to development (and not only to other countries, also to itself), to ecological stability, and to peace. Their analysis would go beyond the problems taken up and answered by the first and second generation, except for the remedial task of interpreting and emphasizing these rights for women, children, other peoples, indigenous or "minorities," both or neither. This quadruple concern for the marginalized, and for development-environment-peace, is today particularly prominent in the green movement, hence the term "green rights." What chances do they have of becoming institutionalized?

In the preceding chapter one point made was that we are no longer on the safe and simple ground of punishing evil actors and/or distributing fairly goods and services like education and health. Essentially the green rights lead us straight to the problem of structural and cultural change, not only intra- but also inter-societally, beyond the classical approaches of punishment and redistribution. Nobody would expect that to be accepted easily by the powers on top of the present structures. We are in for the long haul, with much and creative use of UD:28 (see page 86).

But how long? For the first generation the struggle lasted about one century (mid-eighteenth to mid-nineteenth) and for the second generation one more century – till the mid-twentieth: about the time consciousness about third-generation green rights emerged, first development (1960s), then environment (1970s), and then peace (1980s).[18] In all three cases the technocratic state–capital alliance was and is challenged, for having the wrong ends (growth instead of development, cleaning-up instead of eco-balance, deterrence instead of peace), and for being technically incompetent with the means. So, if past experience is a guide, we should see some transformation by the mid-twenty-first century.[19]

And then what? The conclusion from chapter 1 is obvious: by that time the non-West will have achieved sufficient self-confidence to put an end to the Columbian era of world history and not only demand but gradually achieve a de-Westernization of the human rights tradition to make the rights more universal. One ten-point agenda is given on pages 18–25, consisting partly of structural and partly of cultural items. Such agendas will be written and rewritten all the time.[20] But so far the human rights debate has been essentially intra-societal and intra-Western; concerned with intra-societal problems expressed in a Western discourse. That time is coming to an end.

A metaphor may be useful here. On 10 December 1948 the Universal Declaration of Human Rights came into being, given birth by the United Nations General Assembly. The output reflects well Judeo–Christian culture, including the tendency of that culture to see itself as universal. See this as one stop on a journey, long, possibly endless. There are more stops, new passengers enter, there is a dialogue inside. Maybe some passengers exit. There are more stops and new declarations, each time reflecting an ever deeper and broader *dialogue des civilisations*. Each culture gives something. Each culture is grateful that others have something to contribute. Each culture feels that "if you accept something from me, I'll reciprocate." And as the journey progresses we all benefit from true universality, from universality as a never-ending process involving all cultures.

TOWARD A RAINBOW OF RIGHTS – A DIALOGUE

Instead of a conclusion let us try to write some of this dialectic as a dialogue between four persons: Blue, Red, Green, and Colored (non-white), each of them eagerly emphasizing the greatness of their own generation of rights:

BLUE: All three of you go too far. What I do is to define the minimum human rights as standards for a truly human society, from which we can fan out in all directions. You freeze politics into the shape of human rights, far too many of them, universalizing your own ideologies. I define a minimum state that guarantees the basic conditions for human self-realization. You blow up that state by giving it by far too many tasks.

RED: But you only did half the job! You liberated your own kind of bourgeois people and conveniently forgot the other half, and particularly how the other half dies. Are the working classes not entitled to the same share of the good life as you? You created class society – the freedoms you talk of are fine, but you forgot to see to it that everybody can benefit. To overcome that very strong class structure more rights are needed than your minimum civil rights. Capital will not do that voluntarily. The state is needed.

GREEN: What you two do not understand is how limited your conception is of human society. Not only did you forget women, children and what you call minorities, other peoples. But you identify the country so much with state and capital, including the working classes, not only the leisured classes, that you forgot three other points. First, you forgot so many human beings – women, children, foreigners, etc. – and what is the goal of development if not to make strong people, not only strong countries and strong elites? Second, you forgot nature, the whole environment. And third, you even forgot the world, the interstate system, ravaged by wars.

COLORED: But all three of you assume Western nineteenth-, even late eighteenth-century nation-state structures to be identical with human society; and you assume Western culture, and for that reason the Western debate, to be identical with world culture. You forget that in the world there are other societies that also might like to develop. Development is the unfolding of the potentials in all civilizations, and of civilizations there are certainly more than one. In short, your similarities by far outweigh the differences. Even you, Ms Green, more universalist than those gentlemen, assume that we shall applaud you and your discourse, admittedly more forward-looking, more progressive. But how many greens are interested in Muslim, Hindu, Buddhist, Confucian, Daoist, Shinto values, and in the many indigenous Amerindian, Pacific and African civilizations? We are all humans, we are all inspired by the values of our civilizations. But we all see human rights also in terms of our cultures, not for that reason neglecting Western contributions.

BLUE and RED: What you say might make some sense if the world were one single state. In that case we could talk of human rights as having run full circle, the community of states and the world state being identical. But the world is still an anarchic system of states only partly implementing human rights. Why not first promote these basic human rights, even enshrined in the International Bill of Rights, and then come to your own cultures?

GREEN: And I might like to add: how can I know that your development does not mean repression of women and

	children and other peoples, arguing that "it is in my culture?" Buddhists may respect nature, perhaps also Hindus, but how about the rest? And are your states not every bit as growth-orientated at the expense of people and nature as Western states? And what if war, not peace, is also in your culture?
COLORED:	Well, here we go. All of you emphasize, all the time, an unwritten human right: your right to tell the rest of the world what to do. Mr Blue and Mr Red assume states to be true agents of these rights; Ms Green emphasizes how state and capital stand in the way of their implementation. Imagine we emphasize the right not to live in a Western-style society at all, but prefer small societies based on mutual rights and obligations, state-less, ruled with the consent of the ruled, but based on consensus obtained by dialogues rather than majorities obtained by voting?
BLUE, RED and GREEN:	But how do you guarantee rights of individuals, the pillar of the whole human rights construction?
COLORED:	What if some of us do not believe that there is such a thing as individuals, that individual human beings exist only in a collectivity whose survival implies individual survival?
BLUE:	But the freedom of expression . . .
RED:	The right to gainful employment . . .
GREEN:	The right to a clean environment . . .
COLORED:	All of that is important. Among us there are many ways of looking at it, though. By the way, what about the human rights of anyone in your society who not only preaches but practices a state-less society, refuses to pay taxes, to carry identification, and manages to travel abroad without a passport?
BLUE and RED:	Will be arrested, and rightly so!
GREEN:	I am not so sure . . .
COLORED:	I am not so sure either. All I say is that the political agenda in general, and the human rights agenda in particular, is not exhausted because the West has no more ideas. There could be other ideas elsewhere.
BLUE, RED and GREEN:	Maybe.
COLORED:	And to that Western maybe: Maybe.

NOTES

CHAPTER 1
HUMAN RIGHTS AND THE WESTERN TRADITION

1 "Western" is here interpreted in the sense of "occidental" as opposed to "oriental," not as "Western" as opposed to "Eastern" in "Eastern Europe." "Occidental" is then defined in terms of the three Abrahamitic/Semitic religions: Judaism, Christianity and Islam. Major common characteristics are transcendentalism, trinity (not for Christianity), singularism (monopoly on validity), universalism (universal validity, not for Judaism), individualism (through a detachable and enduring self anchored in the soul) and immortality (through one-way migration of the soul after death; less significant in Judaism). None of these characteristics is found in Hinduism/Buddhism.

2 For this conceptualization of human rights, see J. Galtung and A. Wirak, "Human Needs and Human Rights – A Theoretical Approach", in *Bulletin of Peace Proposals*, 8, 3 (1977), pp. 251–8.

3 See Raimundo Panikkar, "La notion des droits de l'homme, est-elle un concept occidental?", *Diogenes*, 120 (1982), pp. 87–115. Also see Pollis and Schwab, *Human Rights, Cultural and Ideological Perspectives* (New York, Praeger, 1980). It should be noted that the individualism of the Occident, embedded in the concept of the individual soul, is precisely what makes the knots stand out relative to the net in Panikkar's sense whereas the *anatta* (no soul) concept opens for a net rather than a knot perspective. Thus it may be true that only the West has codified, specified the dignity of the individual. But this may also be

close to a tautology because only the West is so extreme in conceiving of the individual as detachable and enduring (the two characteristics denied in the Buddhist *anatta* doctrine). This type of codification would be meaningless in an oriental context if the "Orient" is defined as the part of the world touched by Buddhism. Moreover, what is codified can also be eroded as the West does through excessive fragmentation, destroying the net; by imposing duties outweighing the rights; by exporting such structures as slavery, colonialism, and the harsher aspects of capitalism highly incompatible with the human dignity of others; and by exporting Western ideas of the state coupled with individualistic human rights concepts to cultures where (excessive) individualism is seen as the opposite of dignity.

4   This is, of course a general perspective in transactional analysis; there is a *quid* for every *quo*, a *do* for every *des*. "There is no such thing as a free lunch" is a fruitful analytical perspective in any interactive system, not only a conservative tenet of belief.

5   Characteristically these duties are not spelt out. But art. 29, para. 2 gives a hint:

> In the exercise of his rights and freedoms, everyone shall be subject only to such limitations as are determined by law solely for the purpose of securing due recognition and respect for the rights and freedoms of others and of meeting the just requirements of morality, public order and the general welfare in a democratic society.

These are very soft formulations of what states feel entitled to impose as duties on their citizens. At no point does this mean that the state should not be entitled to define duties. As Gandhi has said: "The Ganges of rights flows from the duties of Himalaya." The point is only that the citizen has a right not only to ask whether the rights/duties balance constitutes a good deal, but to challenge that deal in words and action and demand a new one, even a new social contract. Above all, the citizen has a right to know what the duties are, "determined by law."

6   See J. F. C. Fuller, *The Conduct of War 1789–1961* (London, Eyre Methuen, 1972), Ch. 2, "The rebirth of unlimited war", pp. 26–41. It is unnecessary to share Fuller's views on "human nature," as one-sided and *homo homini lupus*-orientated as the Toynbee view of democracy as something that "breathes the spirit of the Gospels . . . and its motive-force is Love" is romantic. General conscription had predecessors such as "the *Ordinanza* of 1505 [drafted by Machiavelli], the law that established obligatory military service between the ages of 18 and 80 in Florence" (Fuller, p. 32). However, it was the decree of the post-revolutionary Convention in Paris, 23 August 1793, that established general conscription on a basis lasting till our days: "*publions une*

grande verité: la liberté est devenue créancière de tous les citoyens; les uns lui doivent leur industrie, les autres leur fortune, ceux-ci leur conseils, ceux-la leurs bras; tous lui doivent le sang qui coule dans leurs veines" (quoted in Fuller, p. 33). A very clear statement of the reciprocity principle is "to preach the unity of the Republic and hatred against Kings" (Fuller, p. 32). Ekkehart Krippendorff, in his seminal *Staat und Krieg: Die historische Logik politischer Unvernunft* (Frankfurt, Suhrkamp, 1985), goes one step further in ch. 5, "*Wie es in Europa anfing: Krieger auf Staatssuche*", pp. 206–43. His basic point is that the whole state formation was designed to finance armies so expensive that the princes could no longer raise the money (e.g. through commercial loans). Rather than states creating armies for their political security armies created states for their economic security. Part of this picture is how cheap warfare became with general conscription: "Without conscription Napoleon's policy of conquest would have been impossible; in 1805, at Schönbrunn, he boasted to Metternich that he could afford to expend 80,000 a month – men were now so cheap as dirt" (Fuller, p. 35). For the same argument in another context, the answer of Hungary's (then communist) Foreign Minister to a demand for alternative service for conscientious objectors is interesting: "Military service," the Minister went on, was "a duty in return for rights, and the Catholic Church agrees" (*Financial Times*, 25 April 1985).

7 A list of seven major achievements in the US (and the Western democracies in general) would certainly include the rule of law, freedom of movement inside and outside the country, the right to own property, freedom of thought, freedom of expression, freedom of assembly and the right to take part in government. All seven were weak in the Soviet Union, although the situation improved on all of them under *glasnost/perestroika* conditions (what will happen in the successor republics remains to be seen). Seven points on which the Soviet Union used to be proud in the pre-Gorbachev era would include the right to work, sufficient wages for a decent living, the right to rest and leisure, guaranteed basic needs in terms of food/clothing/housing, guaranteed health care, guaranteed education at all levels and the right to take part in culture; all of them weakly developed in the US. For "the US seven" see the Universal Declaration of Human Rights, arts 12, 13, 17, 18, 19, 20, and 21; for "the Soviet Union seven" arts 6, 7a(ii), 7d, 11, 12, 13, and 15a of the International Covenant on Economic, Social and Cultural Rights (16 December 1966). Each Declaration/Convention is also to a large extent present in the other. See A. Rosas and J. Helgesen, *Human Rights in a Changing European Perspective* (London and New York, Pinter Publishers, 1990).

8 For an indication of the approach, see J. Galtung, T. Heiestad and E. Rudeng, "On the last 2,500 years in Western history; and some

reflections on the coming 500", ch. 12 in Peter Burke (ed.), *The New Cambridge Modern History, Companion Volume* (Cambridge, Cambridge University Press, 1978).

9   Those who consider this an argument in favor of a system might consider that most slaves would prefer migration to the slave-owner's house from their own quarters, most serfs would prefer to live in the castle-upon-a-hill, and many concentration camp inmates would have opted in favor of the house of the camp commandant, including a change of occupation in that direction. In none of these cases are we inclined to accept such urges as proof of the legitimacy of the underlying social order. The use of the argument in the international field reveals the lack of ability to recognize structures from social space in the more extended world space.

10   See Christopher D. Stone, *Should Trees Have Standing?* (Los Altos, Kaufmann, 1974).

11   See the approach by Peter Singer in his seminal *Animal Liberation* (London, Cape, 1976). The debate has reached the popular level (from which it also comes), as seen in *Newsweek* articles, "Emptying the cages, does the animal kingdom need a bill of rights?", 23 May 1988, pp. 59–60 and "Of pain and progress", 26 December 1988, pp. 50–9; also see "Animal rights", *The Economist*, 16 November 1991, pp. 25–8.

12   An example might be the Alta hydro-electric power project that became a major issue in Norway in the early 1980s. "*La Elva leve*," let the river live, was a major slogan, expressing the idea of the river as a valid norm-object; for some also a valid norm-subject. In Norway this long-lasting civil disobedience campaign derived its motivation not only from solidarity with the indigenous population, the *sami*, but also from a certain pantheistic tradition.

13   M. S. McDougal, H. D. Lasswell and L. Chen, *Human Rights and World Public Order* (New Haven, Yale University Press, 1980).

Chapter 2
Human Rights and the Legal Tradition

1   For more on this, see J. Galtung, *The True Worlds, A Transnational Perspective* (New York, Free Press/Macmillan, 1980), Ch. 2.1.

2   For an effort to explore this theme, relating it to news communication, see J. Galtung and M. H. Ruge, "The structure of foreign news", *Essays in Peace Research*, vol. IV (Copenhagen, Ejlers, 1977), Ch. 4.

3   One reflection of this asymmetry is found in the rather strong asymmetry between the amount of money, manpower and institution-

building devoted to punishment (fines, imprisonment, etc.) and devoted to rewards (medals, orders, citations).

4 This theme is explored in Ch. 9 of J. Galtung, *Methodology and Ideology* (Copenhagen, Ejlers, 1977).

5 The structural properties of exploitation, penetration/dependency, segmentation, fragmentation, and marginalization are combined into one: imperialism. In a sense this constitutes one possible way of making the idea of "structural violence" – first inspired by my work on Gandhi, in the 1950s (with Arne Naess), then developed in "Violence, peace and peace research", *Essays in Peace Research*, vol. I (Copenhagen, Ejlers, 1975), Ch. 4 – more precise.

6 See "A structural theory of imperialism', *Essays in Peace Research*, vol. IV, Ch. 13 – and particularly in the form it is given in sections 1 and 2 of Ch. 4 of *The True Worlds*.

7 For a discussion of this more explicit version of the legal paradigm, see "Two approaches to disarmament", *Essays in Peace Research*, vol. II, Ch. 3, particularly pp. 56–62.

8 An example: grassroot Palestinian and Israeli reaction to the PLO–Israel agreement signed by Y. Arafat and Y. Rabin in Washington, 13 September 1993.

9 For more details see "Human needs, national interests and world politics: the Law of the Sea Conference", *Essays in Peace Research*, vol. V (Copenhagen, Ejlers, 1978), Ch. 13, pp. 361–80.

10 See J. Galtung, *Development, Environment and Technology* (New York, United Nations, 1979), Part I.

11 See *The True Worlds*, Ch. 2, section 4 "Towards a synthesis" for an effort to combine the two perspectives.

12 These were the figures frequently used during the 50th anniversary of Hilter's *Machtergreifung* in 1933. Note the terrible "efficiency" in the killer/killed ratio.

13 J. Galtung, "Deductive thinking and political practice; an essay on Teutonic intellectual style", *Papers on Methodology* (Copenhagen, Ejlers, 1979), Ch. 8.

14 For instance in Matthew 11: 20–24, ending with (24) "Truly, Sodom will be better off at the Judgment Day than you" (because they hadn't turned to God, 20).

15 Normative and descriptive, values and facts are then not seen dichotomously as mutually exclusive, but more in a yin/yang fashion, meaning that a statement is seen as having normative and descriptive components. More particularly, typical of the purely descriptive is the tendency to change the statement so as to agree with (what is seen as) empirical reality; typical of the purely normative is the tendency to try to change empirical reality so as to agree with the statement (the "norm"). In either case agreement or consonance between the empir-

ical and the verbal is pursued. See J. Galtung, "Expectations and interaction processes", *Inquiry* (1959), pp. 213–34; and "Empiricism, criticism, constructivism: three aspects of scientific activity", in *Methodology and Ideology*, Ch. 2.

16   Anna Christensen, in her "Den juridiska mentaliteten; om mentaliteten och mentalitetsforandringar i en gammal vetenskap", in Pehr Sahlstrom (ed.), *Mentaliteter* (Abo akademi forskningsinstitut, no. 118, pp. 79–90, makes the important point that the legal tradition, like theology, used a normative discourse/language to express its knowledge, not the descriptive discourse that later was to become the clothing in which scientific knowledge was to be verbally dressed. The imperative mode of a verb may (also) be a way of expressing the indicative. A parallel could be drawn to the prophecies of the Prophets where the future tense of a verb (perhaps) was a way of expressing the present. Like Chinese authors using the past as a discourse for the present the Prophets might fear the consequences of present tense, from very present rulers.

17   A point made repeatedly by the Harvard philosopher Wilbur O. Quine, in *From a Logical Point of View*.

18   This may also be a reason, embedded in the deep culture, that so much of the struggle against such major social evils as slavery, colonialism, war, exploitation of workers, of women, of animals, of nature in general has come from England and other countries with this particular normative culture. The basic assumption is that (parts of) the normative culture can be changed and new ones substituted. Obviously, this is also a condition for democracy which presupposes that new (waves of) popular will find their expression through the lawmakers in new laws. The anatomy of pragmatism is detachability of laws, even blocks of laws, from the totality; changing them without critical damage done to the total construction. This way the Anglo-Saxon tradition of "common law" is almost predestined to become a world leader in legal innovation.

19   Thus, the Ten Commandments have survived almost two millennia of gross deviations, with the Catholic priesthood probably knowing more about this than anybody else through the confessions and their mainly verbal sanctions.

20   See J. Galtung and F. Nishimura, "Structure, culture and languages: an essay comparing the Indo-European, Chinese and Japanese languages", *Social Science Information* (1983), pp. 895–925.

21   *Confessio Augustana* (the Lutheran Augsburg Confession from 1530), art. 6.

22   J. Galtung, "Intellectual styles: saxonic, teutonic, gallic, nipponic", in *Methodology and Development* (Copenhagen, Ejlers, 1988), Ch. 1.2, pp. 27–47. As pointed out repeatedly in the article these are ideal

types, like the legal systems. Empirical reality may combine (elements of) these styles. For the same styles in medical theory and practice, see Lynn Payer, *Medicine and Culture* (London, 1988).

23 Thus, René David and J. E. C. Brierley, *Major Legal Systems in the World Today* (New York, Free Press, 1978), see three families of legal systems: "the Romano-Germanic family, the Common law family ('the law of England and those laws modelled on English law') and the family of Socialist law" (p. 21), and then Muslim, Hindu, Jewish, Far East and African law (pp. 27–9). K. Zweigert and H. Kotz, *Einführung in die Rechtsvergleichung* (Tubingen, 1971), divide the systems into Roman, German, Nordic, Anglo-Saxon, Socialist, Far East, Muslim, and Hindu. The World Peace Through Law Center in Washington prepared a pamphlet for World Law Day, 26 August 1973, "Religion and the law", dividing the legal systems into African, Brahmanic, the civil law ("the Roman-Germanic legal tradition"), the common law, the Confucian Order, Islamic law and socialist law. The present chapter comments only on the Anglo-Saxon, Roman, German and one Far East tradition, Japan; leaving out Muslim, Jewish, Hindu, Chinese and African. Socialist law may one day re-emerge.

24 From the fact that they are major UN goals it does, of course, not follow that the human rights approach is adequate for their pursuit. And they had to enter the human rights discourse as "third generation rights", see the second section of chapter 5.

25 The German sayings in this connection are illuminating: *wenn alle das Bose tun hat niemand das getan*; *wenn alle gleich betroffen sind ist niemand betroffen*; *wenn man dem einen Bose bestraft, dann sind 999 freigesprochen*.

26 Of course, this idea also has had catastrophic consequences for non-Western peoples with less of a tradition of private ownership, serving as a justification for "privatizing" what was seen by indigenous people as commonly owned in the sense of being accessible for use by everybody, *with care*.

27 In *A Theory of Civilizations* (forthcoming) this is used as the definition of "cosmology," or the code, in the sense of the deep culture, of a civilization.

28 A deep encounter would be more like work, friendship, love, marriage across cultural borders; not like mass tourism (but possibly cultural tourism) or visits.

29 The Reagan administration in 1982, in the US State Department's *Country Reports on Human Rights Practices for 1982*, dates the human rights movement to 1776: "it is to this historical movement that democratic countries owe their possession of rights, and because of it that other peoples express their yearnings for justice as a demand for rights." The document then goes on to say, in very clear words:

"The human rights activists of the 18th century would thus have said there was a right of individuals to develop, but no right to development" (pp. 3–4; I am indebted to Philip Alston for this reference). What would have happened to the 13 colonies if those human rights activists had argued the right of individuals to independence, for instance from their parents, "but no right to independence?"

30 Some states redistribute surplus they control, some do not; it is not much more complicated than that.

31 One answer is, of course, to do the same as companies and other organizations do: by registering somewhere, including registering their dissolution. The problem can be solved.

32 Examples would include building infrastructure for communication and transport to an isolated group; removal of social stigmas that marginalize a group or excessively violent TV programs that increase violence levels by lowering the violence threshold, thereby marginalizing the group even further. In the same vein, peace can be argued as world development, removing obstacles to equity among nations. Obviously, this condition is very different from peace in the family or with the neighbors, not to mention inner peace of individuals.

33 See J. Donnelly, "International human rights: a regime analysis", *International Organization*, 40, 3 (1986), pp. 599–642. The Commission on Human Rights (of ECOSOC) does norm-creation, promotion and monitoring; the Human Rights Committee (of the General Assembly) does promotion and monitoring; and the Third Committee (also of the GA) does promotion and norm creation. In addition there are working groups and *ad hoc* bodies.

34 Example: in Kerala in 1962 I had occasion to observe that fishermen were of the opinion that fishing nets should only be thrown from one side of the boat. The rule was deemed superstitious by a Norwegian technical assistance team, arguing a double-sided approach. Some functions of the norm are easily identified: to avoid nets getting entangled with one another, to avoid over-fishing. The latter gained in salience over time, but trawlers (introduced by the Norwegians) more than canceled this ancient effort at ecologically compatible behavior.

35 Which is, of course, one recipe for civil disobedience as a form of non-violent resistance against an illegitimate regime.

36 For one analysis of that approach, see J. Galtung, "Functionalism in a new key", Ch. 5 in *Methodology and Ideology*, pp. 131–59.

37 For an excellent analysis of some of the problems with that approach, see G. Meggle, "Grundwerte", in Heike Jung (ed.), *Recht und Moral: Beitrage zu einer Standortbestimmung* (Baden-Baden, Nomos, 1991), pp. 19–37. His analysis focuses on the difficulty in identifying "fundamental/basic" values; the approach here is more in terms of "higher" values. Obviously there are problems. And in a sense that is

good, for otherwise an important debate would freeze into some type of scholasticism.

38   For one elementary presentation of Buddhist tenets of faith, see J. Galtung, *Buddhism: A Quest for Unity and Peace* (Sri Lanka, Sarvodaya Vishva Lekha, 1993). For another approach to comparing rights and needs, see H. Shue, *Basic Needs, Basic Rights, Human Rights in US Foreign Polity* (New York, 1980).

39   Apathetic people are not trouble-makers although their apathy may show up in low economic growth rates. Unrest is what makes a society "ungovernable" according to this thinking.

40   Again, in non-violence theory this is known as passive and active civil disobedience.

CHAPTER 3
HUMAN RIGHTS AND HUMAN NEEDS

1   This position, as can be seen from table 3.2 and figure 3.3, is not unreasonable if "human rights" is interpreted to mean "civil and political rights," the "first generation" in other words.

2   For efforts to discuss, critically and constructively, the concept, the philosophy and the social science of basic human needs, see K. Lederer, J. Galtung and D. Antal (eds), *Human Needs; A Contribution to the Current Debate* (Cambridge, Mass., Oelgeschlager, Gunn and Hain, 1980); including the chapter by the present author, "The basic needs approach", pp. 55–125. For those who are committed to Maslow and his hierarchy of needs, arguments against creating a hierarchy are given on pp. 67–71.

3   This concept would actually include the subconscious. It is assumed that needs are bio-physiological and socio-cultural in their origins and that they differ from values in general because of the consequences of non-satisfaction: a deep state of dis-ease, even disintegration, that may show up at the intra-personal, inter-personal or societal levels, as apathy and/or as rebellion.

4   See Galtung, "The basic needs approach", pp. 62–7. Since that was written I have preferred to change "security" to "survival" and "welfare" to "well-being," the former because "security" actually applies to all classes of needs and come close to sustainability, and "welfare" is too close to one particular institution, the welfare state.

5   The approaches differ significantly: the evil actor is incapacitated, the wrong structure is changed (see the opening section of chapter 2). But there is also the hope that the evil actor will change his or her evil ways, and that the wrong structure will become incapable of operating, by

being paralyzed through strikes and other forms of non-cooperation/ civil disobedience.

6   This approach to social norms is elaborated in J. Galtung, *Norm, Role and Status: A Synthetic Approach to Social Structure* (Santiago, FLACSO, 1962), mimeo, unpublished.

7   In fact, the entire society, national and global, is interwoven with such norm-triads in all kinds of directions. If they materialized as strings we would be as unable to move as we would were radio waves more like ocean waves. If things do not develop as they should it is hardly for lack of norms, nor necessarily because of their content, but because of the composition of the norm-triads.

8   Or more precisely: the social micro level, including such units as families and households where that would be a more proper way of reflecting social reality.

9   See J. Galtung, "On alpha and beta and their many combinations", in J. Galtung and E. Masini (eds), *Visiones de sociedades deseables* (Mexico, Cesteem, 1979) (in Spanish).

10   This paradigm is explored in some detail in J. Galtung, "Two approaches to disarmament: the legalist and the structuralist", *Essays in Peace Research*, vol. II (Ejlers, Copenhagen, 1976), pp. 54–93, particularly pp. 58ff.

11   This does not mean that science is only based on that idea. If the thesis is sufficiently important and sufficiently centrally located in a theory it will not be given up that easily; it attains normative character. See J. Galtung, "Empiricism, criticism, constructivism: three aspects of scientific activity", in *Methodology and Ideology*, pp. 41–71.

12   This again refers to the first generation of human rights.

13   Remember the Arab saying: "A camel is a horse as designed by a committee."

14   Just as there are (at least) two concepts of freedom – freedom *from* constraint, and freedom to develop further; the first being a freedom *to* choose among known options, the second the freedom to develop that range of options further – there may also be (at least) two concepts of repression. On the one hand there is reduction of action-space already conquered; on the other hand the failure to be elastic enough to permit expansion of action-spaces further. A society may be repressive in none, either or both senses.

15   In zoos both survival and well-being in the sense of food, clothes and shelter are taken care of; even health and some education; freedom and identity not. In many respects like the European socialist countries.

16   If this were not the case there would not be that much dissatisfaction with the welfare state; ultimately leading to its partial dismantling even in stronghold Nordic countries in the 1990s.

17 See J. Galtung, R. Preiswerk and P. O'Brien, *Self-Reliance* (London, Bougle L'ouverture, 1980).

18 The famous phrase from *The Godfather*. I am indebted to Immanuel Wallerstein for this image.

19 See F. M. Lappe and J. Collins, *Food First, Beyond the Myth of Scarcity* (Boston, Houghton Mifflin, 1977) and Susan George, *How the Other Half Dies* (London, Penguin, 1976).

20 The procedure has not been that systematic, however – the major purpose of the list is to serve as a heuristic to facilitate the type of analysis given in this book.

21 US Blacks travelling in the South had to plan their itineraries so as not to be blocked by "Whites Only" restrooms; in South Africa this was and is a key problem; for the tourist in a foreign city it may be a source of extreme discomfort.

22 This is the reason Illich developed the thesis that everybody should be entitled not to be schooled, and not to be discriminated against (e.g. in connection with applications for jobs) for lack of schooling, in *Deschooling Society* (New York, Harper & Row, 1971).

23 UD:19 uses the word "media" ("to seek, receive and impart information and ideas through any media"), which can be given a broad and a narrow definition. The right to seek others to obtain their ideas may be said to be more important than the right to look at TV, listen to radio and read newspapers; because it leads to dialogue, to mutual exploration as opposed to one-way communication.

24 For a distinction between two types of countervailing power – power over others and power over oneself – see J. Galtung, *The True Worlds, A Transnational Perspective* (New York, Macmillan, 1980), Ch. 2.4.

25 "To vote and to be elected at genuine periodic elections which shall be by universal and equal suffrage and shall be held by secret ballot, guaranteeing the free expression of the will of the electors." Are we so convinced that this version of Western loneliness and individualism, a political act with the individual confined to a closed booth once every four years or so, is the ultimate answer to the question how "to take part in the conduct of public affairs?" Thus, is it better than a town meeting at irregular intervals, with open discussion? The latter gives advantage to the people able to verbalize, and there may be restraints on the free expression of opinion for fear of the consequences. But the former is such a pallid and easily manipulable, almost *reductio ad absurdum* of politics. Perhaps both, in some combination, should be protected in an International Covenant on Civil and Political Rights?

26 This is one way of formulating a *way of life*. The basic distinction is between dominant and alternative ways of life, the dominant way of life not necessarily being the statistically most frequent (society may not be efficient enough in molding everybody the same way), or necessarily

the way of life of the dominant classes (they will tend to work out more pleasant alternatives for themselves), but the way of life the social structure would tend to facilitate and reward. Human rights of this kind may tend to standardize ways of life in direction of the dominant way far beyond what is healthy for a society that wants to develop options for the future. Obviously, each alternative way of life is a potential future dominant way of life.

27   Thus, UD:26(3) says: "Parents have a prior right to choose the kind of education that shall be given to their children." Read as a right that entitles parents to make the choice as against other adults (the state, the Church, the party) it protects the parents; read as a right that gives this choice to the parents rather than to the children it can be seen as directed against children. This right probably has a rather short life expectancy.

28   The designer has this right, not the worker, a typical expression of class society at work.

29   This was brought up at the Third Bertrand Russell Tribunal about human rights in the Federal Republic of Germany, March 1978, referring to the investigations in connection with the *Radikalenerlass*.

30   In one sense this is not so strange: humankind has thousands of years of experience with law, one generation at most with data banks.

31   It is interesting to speculate what would be the implications if for "nationality" in article 15 – "(1) Everyone has the right to a nationality. (2) No one shall be arbitrarily deprived of his nationality nor denied the right to change his nationality." – we substitute the words "gender," "generation," "class," "race," etc.

32   This is explored in J. Galtung, "Social outer limits", paper for UNEP, Nairobi, 1977 (unpublished).

33   This is a major reason that definitions of class formation should include ownership of control over means of *intellectual* production, given the ever increasing role of research in a modern production function for goods and services.

34   No doubt there is an element of *Naturrecht* in this: an effort to ground rights in needs, at the same time claiming that needs are not freely chosen values but have an empirical basis because of the empirically verifiable consequences when needs are not met. Why not? Is there a better basis than what serves, or at least does not do disservice to, human beings in particular or life in general extending the needs concept to all sentient life? See J. Galtung, *Buddhism: A Quest for Unity and Peace* (Colombo, Sarvodaya Vishva Lekha, 1993), Ch. 3, pp. 53–82.

35   See Professor Otto Klineberg, "Human needs: a social-psychological approach", Ch. 1, in *Human Needs* (see note 2, above), pp. 19–35.

36   Of these limits we probably know little, only that there are limits of

compassion in *time* (we may be interested in the living conditions of our own children; but what about their children?), *space* (we may be interested in the living conditions of our neighbors, but what about their neighbors?), and *social space* (we may be interested in our own kind, defined by ascription or achievement, but what about the other kind?). All the research on social distance from Bogardus, on social discrimination of all kinds, would seem to indicate that the famous UD:1 is a pious wish, a litany. But again, why not?

37 Thus *social justice* is when the sex ratios at all levels of education are the same as in society at large; *equality* when all have the same level of education; and *equality of access* is social justice in connection with the entry to an institution offering social goods or services. Equality implies social justice but not vice versa. Equality of access (*"Chancengleich-heit"*) is a form of social justice, and does not imply equality (after access they may get more or less out of it, for instance by being male and/or upper class).

38 Alternative, more liberal, broader formulations might be needed here, like "everyone is entitled to live together with and establish a household with the persons of his and her choice"; in other words a freedom of association at the level of "living together" and "running a household."

39 Henry Murray, perhaps the first needs theoretician, operates with 28 needs, among them to gain possessions and property (Hilgard and Atkinson, *Introduction to Psychology*, 4th edn, 1967).

40 Needs theory is not a theory of social structure in general, and power in particular, nor should it pretend to be. The theory is intrapersonal, with ramifications at the interpersonal and societal levels.

41 Robert Redfield's *The Little Community* (Chicago, University of Chicago Press, 1960) is such a fine presentation in a broad time–space perspective.

42 For one analysis, see J. Galtung, *Towards Self-Reliance and Global Interdependence* (Ottawa, CIDA, 1978).

43 See, for instance, J. Galtung, "The new international order and the basic needs approaches", *Alternatives*, IV, (1978/79), pp. 455–76.

44 In other words, a clear case whereby a collective *right* may stand in the way of an individual *need*.

45 See the chapter "Poor countries vs. rich; poor people vs. rich; whom will NIEO benefit?", in Galtung, *Towards Self-Reliance* (note 42, above).

46 This presupposes a view of history according to which the Western way of doing things is spreading outward, even to the point that it may leave the old centers (such as London) and take root in new ones elsewhere. (e.g. Sao Paulo, Lagos, Riyadh, Tehran, Singapore, Hong Kong, Taipeh, Seoul and Tokyo).

47   The assumption, then, is that NIEO to be operative will have to reproduce the exploitation so important in the Old International Economic Order, but as the First World countries will resist being objects of exploitation they will turn elsewhere; to the poor populations of their own countries (conservative policies) or to the new Third World, the former socialist countries.

48   See the excellent paper by Peider Konz, "Human rights in the context of development", prepared for the United Nations University, April 1977, with a very subtle approach to such topics as the rights to health, cultural identity (clean, safe, healthy), environment and human rights relating to cybernetics and computer technology, implications of molecular biology and genetic engineering, and justice and security in rapidly growing urban settings.

49   Thus, if satisfaction of needs is a *conditio sine qua non* for human beings to function, this begs the question: What are the necessary conditions for the satisfiers of the needs to be available? It should be pointed out that questions in terms of necessary conditions do not reveal a commitment to functionalism as this was originally conceived (1) because the question may lead to a range of alternative answers, not just the one that is institutionalized in a given society, (2) because there is no assumption that any given order should be preserved. The assumption would be that human beings should be preserved. And that is the reason needs are here conceived of as *human* needs.

50   If this were not the case it would be the end of national sovereignty.

51   This is an application of the old Durkheimian principle or "law" that deviants from norms are needed to demonstrate what the norm is about; in other words, pedagogically, and to test and develop further the enforcement machinery.

52   The Final Act of the Helsinki Conference in 1975 was used this way in the ex-socialist countries of Eastern Europe and the Soviet Union, as is well known. For one analysis, see Martin Kriele, *Die Menschenrechte zwischen Ost und West* (Köln, von Nottbeck, 1977).

53   Thus, one might like more explicit consideration of this in the formulation of the human rights relating to education.

54   See Galtung, "The basic needs approach" (note 2, above), section 5(10).

55   For one analysis, see J. Galtung and D. Poleszynski, *Health and Development*, Ch. 4 "Culture, structure and mental disorder" (forthcoming).

56   Of course, public debate in many countries, coordinated by movements and conferences and declarations, helps considerably. It is through fight and struggle that new rights gain acceptance. But what happens is often that others work out the rights without any consultation with

those whose struggle made it politically possible; sometimes also deliberately deceiving them.

57 This is a basic paradigm for the satisfier/need (or means/ends) relationships, rather common sense, but so often neglected. If something works up to a point, why should not twice as much of it work at least twice as well? It may do so, but only up to a certain point and then it becomes counterproductive or at least non-productive.

58 Thus, in terms of figure 3.1, the argument would be to strengthen the triads that show up as more horizontal, lower-level lines in the diagram.

59 See chapter 2: "Is the legal tradition structure-blind?".

60 And even if it could be shown that somebody had designed a particularly alienating work structure, and had intended to do so, would there be a legal case against him or her if the level of somatic damage was not higher, perhaps even lower, than usual? The basic point seems to be that we have still not come around to taking mental and spiritual phenomena seriously.

61 Thus, one would not hold against a person that he or she does not initiate an action that would be a sufficient condition for higher levels of welfare and identity. The approach is proscriptive rather than prescriptive: do not stand in the way of conditions for needs-satisfaction! To guarantee work satisfaction may be problematic, but if a particular work structure (usually exemplified by the assembly line) can be shown to be a sufficient condition for dissatisfaction, then its removal is a necessary condition for satisfaction and there is basis for action, and for human rights formation.

CHAPTER 4
HUMAN RIGHTS AND SOCIAL STRUCTURES

1. For the author's ideas about development, see A Theory of Development, forthcoming.

2 This section is an outcome of discussions in the Goals, Processes and Indicators of Development Project (of the United Nations University).

3 See J. Galtung and D. Poleszynski, Health and Development, Ch. 4, "Culture, structure and mental disorder" (forthcoming).

4 See the quarterly journal Torture, from the International Rehabilitation Center for Torture Victims, Copenhagen.

5 Whether this is due to the CFCs, space ships, etc. burning holes and leaving gases behind, or both, or other causes.

6 Whether this in fact is happening or not, and due to greenhouse gases or not; the phenomenon figures on anybody's list.

7 Inclusion of human overpopulation as pollution/depletion may be

objectionable; as disturbing whatever ecological balance existed before, perhaps less so if balance is seen as a human–environment relationship. From Mother Gaia's point of view the classification of human as pollution seems more reasonable. From an anthropocentric point of view Mother Gaia is "limited" so there are "limits to growth," meaning for human beings.

8   See J. Galtung, "Cultural violence", *Journal of Peace Research*, 27, 3 (1990), pp. 291–305.

9   The Chinese refer to this as *rezhi* vs. *fazhi*. For an interesting essay relating this to Chinese social change in the 1980s see article in *Time*, 19 December 1988, pointing out that "the number of Chinese lawyers has soared from a scant 2,000 in 1980 to 25,000 today." However, "due process is still applied capriciously." That *rezhi* and *fazhi* do not exclude each other but relate to each other in a yin/yang fashion, with "rule of men" also within due process, and, usually unspoken, due process in "the rule of men" goes without saying.

10   For an example of how this can be done historically, see David E. Stannard, *American Holocaust* (New York/Oxford, Oxford University Press, 1992), tracing the genocide by Europeans (later Americans) on the peoples of the Western Hemisphere essentially back to Christianity. For an effort to trace crimes of this century back to deep culture, see my own *Hitlerism, Stalinism, Reaganism: Three Variations on a Theme by Orwell* (English editions forthcoming), in the Norwegian, Spanish and German editions (Oslo, Gyldendal, 1984; Alicante, Gil Albert, 1985; Baden-Baden, Nomos, 1987).

CHAPTER 5
HUMAN RIGHTS AND SOCIAL PROCESSES

1   The four largest TNCs (and their assets) are Royal Dutch Shell ($69 billion), Ford Motor Company ($55 billion), General Motors Corporation ($52 billion) and IBM ($46 billion): *Development and Cooperation*, 5 (1993), editorial by Dieter Brauer.

2   The four largest INGOs are the International Co-operative Alliance (663 million members in 86 countries), International Federation of Red Cross and Red Crescent Societies (250 million in 117 countries), World Federation of Trade Unions (175 million in 85 countries) and International Federation of Free Trade Unions (113 million in 117 countries): from Union of International Associations, Brussels.

3   The largest countries in the world according to population are, of course, China (estimates seem to vary between 1,140 and 1,200 million) and India (estimates vary between 860 and 890 million). With the much

higher birth rate in India than in China India will pass China some time before 2050.

4 Following the Brandt Commission (on development), the Palme Commission (on security) and the Brundtland Commission (on the environment) the Commission on Global Governance, co-chaired by Ingvar Carlsson and Shridath Ramphal, is trying to come to grips with exactly that problem.

5 For an argument that the European civil society in general and the dissident and peace movements in particular, certainly with Gorbachev from the state system, brought about the end of the Cold War, see J. Galtung, "Eastern Europe 1989 – what happened, and why?", *Research in Social Movements, Conflicts and Change*, 14 (1992), pp. 75–97.

6 Major forms of violation, indeed rampant, are torture, detention of political dissidents, and repression and exploitation of peoples within their borders; the victims being minorities, indigenous, both or neither. Amnesty International has identified over 60 governments as guilty of using torture as a systematic way of oppressing people, and an equal number of governments as indulging in torture now and then. This terrible testimony to the cruelty of the state system is evident in, among other places, the Rehabilitation Center for Torture Victims, in Copenhagen under the dynamic leadership of Dr Inge Kemp Genefke.

   Newsweek, in an excellent overview ("The prisoners of conscience", 14 February 1983), and countless other newspaper and magazine articles for that matter, reveal the workings of the state system: "Nearly one-half of the 157 members of the United Nations hold political prisoners of one sort or another: those of conscience jailed for their beliefs; those whose convictions have driven them to directly challenge their governments." Amnesty International is rightly eulogized in the article, whereas the magazine's home country comes out badly: "So far, however, no US policy, quiet or loud, has made much of a dent in the world's political-prisoner population." Of course not, as a leading member of the state system, even a hegemonial power (some might say: the hegemons' hegemon) interest in stability in the state system would make the US condone, even actively support, such violations inside its own system. The basic point is that political police, torture and detention are as much parts of the state system as the military, wars and arms races. And even if the state does not directly commit these crimes it may omit to stop them by failing to control police, militia, security forces, death squads; in a sense an obvious state strategy as response to the unaccustomed internal intervention brought about by the human rights regime.

7 Where would the human rights tradition have been today without Amnesty International? And, of course, not only Amnesty, but also

the Helsinki Watch, Asia Watch, Africa Watch, Middle-East Watch system; people's tribunals like the Bertrand Russell Tribunals (the first was about Vietnam and pitted one French giant against another when de Gaulle said to Sartre, "*vous ne pouvez pas juger des états!*"); Indian organizations like the People's Union for Democratic Rights, and the People's Union for Civil Liberties, and so on, and so forth.

8   Such efforts at "humanitarian assistance" may be seen as just that, as humanitarian assistance; as when police violate the sacredness of family privacy, prompted by reports about child abuse, battered women, etc. But "humanitarian assistance" can also be seen in at least two other perspectives: as forcing lesser states in a hegemonial system to submit to the hegemons, with human rights legitimacy from the UN, and as ways of showing the world civil society where the ultimate power is located: in the world state system.

9   The argument can, of course, be made that banks brought the states into existence much more than vice versa, for instance by financing their incessant warfare.

10 Chadwick F. Alger, "Actual and potential roles for NGOs in world-wide movements for the attainment of human rights", *Transnational Associations*, 6 (1992), pp. 320–32. Alger compares the work of NGOs in connection with the infant formula marketing code, the right of labor to strike in Guatemala, apartheid in South Africa and church anti-militarism in Latin America.

11 Thus, human rights are very powerful tools in transition periods, such as 1688 (the "glorious" revolution in England), the 1770–90 period (US and France, and the general rise of the bourgeoisie), and indeed now with the whole world system in turmoil. Emerging human rights are the rights of emerging elites, and as they become ruling elites those rights become ruling human rights and will be used as arguments against a new generation of emerging rights. This is the argument of the next section. Incidentally, George Jellineck, in *La Déclaration des Droits de l'homme et du Citoyen* (Paris, Fontemoing, 1902), makes the point, very strongly, that the French Declaration of 26 August 1789 was not inspired by Rousseau's *contrat social* but by the "bill of rights" of the American colonies.

12 One more case of the ambiguity of the state and the state system. Wars may victimize entire populations and leave the country in ruins; those who are supposed to deter and defend, the armies, may be equally or more victimized. And then they may also, in some cases, function legitimately, deterring and in the worst case defending their country.

13 "Other peoples" may then include indigenous populations, ethnic minorities (or majorities for that matter), migrant workers, in classical Europe Jews and Moors, and others.

14 Thus, deposed clergy may reincarnate socially as intellectuals, pro-

fessionals and artists and deposed aristocrats as bureaucrats and corporate executives. For absolute monarchs the situation is more problematic, except as constitutional monarchs. No reincarnation if nirvana has been reached, to stay with the metaphor, with villas in Estoril (outside Lisboa) as nirvana.

15 Of course there are parallels: nationality and property are something people have. But there are also significant differences. Sociologically nationality is ascribed at birth, whether by *ius sanguinis* or *ius solis*, whereas property is acquired through inheritance or achieved during the life span. However, the right to have property and to use property to acquire more property is at the root of liberal-capitalist society so we would expect this to be enshrined in the basic instrument of human rights.

16 In other words, not only lack of high status (layers 1 and 2) or lack of property shall stand in the way of acquiring property.

17 And nevertheless there is a basic problem: the non-ratification by the US (Senate) of major instruments of human rights. This is serious since the US is a major norm-sender in general in the world and in addition sees itself and is seen by others as a stronghold for the human rights tradition. To be a non-sender of these norms, which is what non-ratification amounts to, creates a situation filled with ambiguity, leading some doubt the validity of the entire second generation, legitimizing others who do not want to live up to those obligations anyhow, and still others to doubt the US in general and the executive and the Senate in particular. Thus, the following instruments remain non-ratified (including several whose content specifies first-generation rights for special groups, or which have norm-senders different from the UN): the International Covenant on Economic, Social and Cultural Rights (ICESCR); the International Covenant on Civil and Political Rights (ICCPR), Optional Protocol which entitles citizens to bring complaints against their own government (the rest of the Convention was ratified at the end of the Bush administration, 1992); the Convention against Torture and Cruel, Inhuman or Degrading Treatment or Punishment (Convention against Torture); the Convention on the Elimination of All Forms of Racial Discrimination (Race Convention); the Convention on the Elimination of All Forms of Discrimination Against Women (Women's Rights Convention); The UN Convention of the Rights of the Child (Children's Rights Convention, adopted by the UN, 20 November 1989); the American Convention on Human Rights (American Convention) and the ILO Convention Concerning Indigenous and Tribal Peoples in Independent Countries (adopted by the General Conference, 27 June, 1989).

One US argument against ICESCR, which tries to establish universal rights to secondary education, gainful employment, healthy working conditions, and recognized holidays and vacation time, has been that "the idea of economic and social rights is easily abused by repressive governments" that might be tempted to put off granting basic individual liberties at the same time (Elliott Abrams, then Assistant Secretary of State for Human Rights and Humanitarian Affairs, in *International Herald Tribune*, 11 February 1982). No doubt there is something to this argument; socialist countries may be accused of having done exactly that. To Abrams these were aspirational rights, something achievable only in the long run, whereas civil and political rights are not "something that should come along the road to development some decade."

But the issue is probably much deeper. If the essence of human rights is already enshrined in the 1776 US Declaration of Independence, and there is no mention of ICESCR rights, that already invalidates them to some. Moreover, such rights would interfere with two basic pillars of the US socio-cultural construction: the *market*, by imposing restraints on the economic activity both of buyers and sellers, of labor and of products; and *God*, who might regard how people fare economically as an indicator of how they fare morally. ICESCR would steer God's finger.

In addition, all these instruments might give the state system too much of a hold on the US, reducing freedom of action, increasing complex foreign entanglements. But ultimately ratification will come, perhaps during the Clinton administration?

18 The UNGA reciprocated, acknowledging the trends, by adopting a "Declaration of the Right to Development" in 1986, a "Declaration of the Right of Peoples to Peace" in 1984, and endorsed the Stockholm "Declaration on the Human Environment" in 1972.

19 And that would be for a new generation of human rights, again with the prediction that the US might be among the very last to ratify; if past experience is a guide. Thus, it took the US 40 years to ratify the international convention outlawing genocide (the Genocide Convention), adopted by the UN in 1948, ratified by the US Senate in 1988, eagerly promoted by Senator Proxmire. Ratification was held up for six years by Senator Thurmond, who insisted that the corresponding new US law call for capital punishment. However, as usual there is a deeper level of opposition: "Some conservatives in Congress had opposed the treaty on the grounds that its definition of genocide might encourage American Indians to sue the United States Government for their suffering earlier in the nation's history and also that it might result in unsubstantiated charges being brought against the United States by present-day adversaries" (*New York Times*, 15 October 1988).

20 Thus, on page 104 a list of 15 human rights candidates is suggested as a result of looking into the needs/rights interface. In the final section of

chapter 4 there is an implicit list with one over-arching heading: *the right to live in (social and world) structures that do not continuously produce and reproduce maldevelopment, eco-deterioration and peace-lessness*. To this could be added the inalienable right to withdraw from such structures (a sub-right here would be a human right to conscientious objection to military service), and the right to live in structures that are transparent (No. 10 on the list on page 104) so that people in general know more or less not only what is going on but what is being planned. The latter is problematic since both the world state system and the world corporate system are based on some element of secrecy, particularly by states planning military aggression, and corporations economic aggression, on someone else. Again, there is more than enough to do. For an excellent introduction to the political philosophies underlying these struggles for power and generations of rights, see Will Kymlicka, *Contemporary Political Philosophy* (Oxford, Clarendon Press, 1990), analyzing utilitarianism, liberal equality, libertarianism, Marxism, communitarianism and feminism. An additional chapter on Gandhism would have been appropriate.

INDEX

Lightning Source UK Ltd.
Milton Keynes UK
UKOW06f1151260515

252290UK00001B/231/P